Renewing Democracy in Young America

Renewing Democracy
in Young America

DANIEL HART AND JAMES YOUNISS

OXFORD
UNIVERSITY PRESS

Oxford University Press is a department of the University of Oxford. It furthers
the University's objective of excellence in research, scholarship, and education
by publishing worldwide. Oxford is a registered trade mark of Oxford University
Press in the UK and certain other countries.

Published in the United States of America by Oxford University Press
198 Madison Avenue, New York, NY 10016, United States of America.

CIP data is on file at the Library of Congress
ISBN 978-0-19-064151-1 (pbk.)
ISBN 978-0-19-064148-1 (hbk.)

9 8 7 6 5 4 3 2 1

Paperback printed by WebCom, Inc., Canada
Hardback printed by Bridgeport National Bindery, Inc., United States of America

CONTENTS

We began this book in 1994. Not the writing—though the project has moved so gradually that at times it has felt like the initial outline dated back to then—but our two decades of discussion concerning young people and their places in the world. Our conversation began in 1994 when Youniss invited Hart to spend parts of his sabbatical at the Catholic University of America. Twenty years of evolving discussion, findings from our own work and that of others, substantial changes in the demographics of the United States, and shifts in popular culture led us to judge that the time was right to offer our views about how best to support young people as they enter into and assume responsibility for democratic civic life in the United States.

Our conversations and the shape of this book have been structured by a fascination with the negotiations of youth with societal institutions. We have studied children and teenagers as they interact with their communities, and our appreciation has grown for the responsiveness of youthful civic dispositions to community experiences. One of our goals for the book is to communicate both the possibility of and responsibility for the promotion of civic development. We want readers—civic educators, policymakers, scholars, and concerned citizens—to act on the fact that civic identities are acquired through experiences: those of us who manage resources can help direct youth's citizenship development. Preparing youth for civic life not only helps them flourish as human beings but strengthens the foundations of human societies. As Katharine Lenroot, head of the Children's Bureau under Franklin Roosevelt, wrote:

> "Youth must find itself in achievement, but it must also lose itself in service. The test of American civilization . . . is the extent to which it offers to youth . . . the stuff from which ideals may be fashioned, and the opportunity for brave endeavor to weave them into the fabric of life" (quoted in Hanna, 1934, p. 267).

Civic life occurs in cultures and political contexts that evolve over time, and each intersection of human development with cultural and political moments raises unique questions, precluding a single, eternal answer. In this book, we do our best to answer questions about how best to support youth's civic development at the beginning of the 21st century. Our efforts to provide answers about advancing civic development draw on social science. As we shall see, social science does not conclusively demonstrate how best to ease youth into civic life. What social science research on civic development offers might be called "stubborn facts," patterns of findings that emerge time and again from well-designed studies. Sometimes these stubborn facts constrain theory and practice. For example, evidence suggests that traditional high school civics classes are surprisingly ineffective in promoting the acquisition of civic knowledge. Thoughtful people can disagree about the implications of this fact—some may advocate for new teaching methods, others for enhanced professional development for teachers, and so on—but there should be consensus that exhorting civics teachers to do more of what they're doing already will not enhance development of competent citizens.

Chapters 5 and 6 offer suggestions for promoting civic development that more closely connect what is done in schools with ongoing civic life in local communities. Our proposals draw on suggestive social science findings about the sources of civic development and are offered in light of the evidence about civic development that is described in chapter 4. We believe that our proposals are grounded in sound theory and have potential, but we acknowledge that future research is needed to reinforce our ideas. We realize also that there are other effective strategies, and we hope that this book encourages further efforts in this vein.

Each of us has studied children and teenagers who have grown up in some of the poorest communities in the United States. No doubt some are damaged by the hardships they endure. Removing the obstacles youth in such communities face ought to be a central aspiration of any ethical society. Yet we have seen time and again youth flourish in even the most difficult circumstances, both thriving and contributing to the civic vitality of their communities. Oftentimes this success is made possible by support from institutions and relationships in the communities. And this observation gives the present book its major theme: when youth are provided with resources and opportunities to contribute to society, they usually respond positively, thereby benefiting both themselves and society. That is why, instead of bemoaning the present state of politics (which we review in chapter 2), we turn to youth who with proper preparation may be able to refresh our democracy and sustain it though the foreseeable future.

Our research has been supported by the William T. Grant Foundation, the Carnegie Corporation of New York, the Fetzer Institute, the Jacobs Foundation, the Radcliffe Institute for Advanced Studies, the Spencer Foundation, and The Robert Wood Johnson Foundation. Daniel Hart is particularly grateful to Rutgers University for its support of his research and youth development work. James Youniss is equally thankful to his students and colleagues at the Catholic University of America who encouraged his scholarly efforts over the decades. We have benefited enormously from conversations with colleagues from several disciplines whose ideas have permeated our own thinking and reappear throughout this book as a testament to what collaborative science should be. We cannot name them all, but those who read outlines and chapters of this book and offered comments include Peter Levine, Joseph Kahne, Joel Westheimer, Marc Hooghe, Ben Kirshner, Constance Flanagan, Andrew Yeo, Matt Green, Charlotte Markey, Ed Metz, Robert Horne, Hugh McIntosh, Robert Atkins, Jeff McLellan, and Richard Berman.

We are particularly grateful for the support of our families and friends.

Dan would like to thank Robert Atkins for his twenty-year partnership in civic development programs and his even longer friendship—it's been an adventure and a pleasure! Charlotte, Dan's wife, has contributed to his thinking about civic development and his appreciation for life—thank you! Finally, Dan thanks those who shared with him their lives as children and youth—Matt, Sarah, Abdoulaye, Dan, Sayla, Olivia—and affirming for him in a personal way how succeeding generations can invigorate American society.

And Jim thanks Dorothy for her smile and support.

Renewing Democracy in Young America

Young America and Democracy

On Friday, January 20, 2017, Donald J. Trump assumed the presidency of the United States of America. A day later, four million Americans—the largest political protest ever recorded in American history (Frostenson, 2017)—gathered around the country in opposition to the policies the new president proposed to enact. Most Americans understood the new president's record low popularity and the widespread public opposition to his initial actions in office to reflect in part the political divisiveness of the times. The vast majority (86%) of Americans believed their country to be more deeply divided than ever before (Pew Research Center, 2017). Only one in four American adults imagined that polarization would soon diminish (Pew Research Center, 2017). Most Americans foresaw continued animosity between political parties in Washington (Pew Research Center, 2017) and, consequently, continued dysfunction in the federal government.

Some of those opposed to the new president blamed young people for his election. Polls indicated that by a substantial margin young people preferred

President Trump's opponent in the election, Hillary Clinton. Projections suggested that if only the votes of those between ages 18 and 29 counted in the election, Clinton would have won by a landslide (Purtill, 2016). Why did the preference for Clinton among young voters not result in her election to the presidency? One reason, of course, is that older voters liked Trump much better than young people did. But another reason is that not enough young people eligible to vote did so. One estimate was that about one million young people who had voted in 2012, and were eligible to vote in the presidential election of 2016, did not do so (Purtrill, 2016). If these young people had gone to the polls and cast their votes for Clinton it is possible that she, rather than Trump, would have won the presidency. Because their voting rates are low, youths' interests may not be reflected in electoral results. Quite understandably, those who want the preferences of young voters to be considered by those who govern want a higher percentage of youth to vote.

Low levels of voting is just one symptom of youth disengagement; young people do not want to run for political office, either. Shames (2017) interviewed hundreds of young people pursuing degrees in law or public policy, two traditional paths to political office, and found that few wanted to work for the government. Many of those Shames interviewed believed that government is ineffective and so riven by ideological division that policy cannot be implemented. Lawless and Fox (2015) surveyed thousands of young people and found that few aspired to work in government. For example, young people asked to choose between being a business executive and a member of Congress—even if the two jobs pay the same— preferred the former by a three-to-one ratio.

Recent headlines even claim that young people may not care much for democracy itself. In *Bloomburg View* an article begins, "Democracy Turns Off Millennials" (Bershidsky, 2016), and another headline in the *Guardian* asks "Have Millennials Given Up on Democracy?" (Safi, 2016). These headlines are based on findings from Foa and Mounk (2016), who analyzed responses to an international survey item, "How essential is it to live in a democracy?" with responses ranging from 1 ("not at all important") to 10 ("absolutely important"). They found that the percentage of people who responded with a 10—that it was "absolutely important"—to live in a democracy declined by generation. For example, while 70% of Americans born in the 1930s reported that it was absolutely important, only about 30% of millennials, born in the 1980s, shared the same view. A similar but less pronounced generational trend was observed in European countries. The findings went "viral" (Voeten, 2016), which suggests the public is ready to doubt the commitment to democracy among young people (even though reanalysis of the same data by Voeten [2016] suggested substantially less decline by generation than proposed by Foa and Mounk).

The 2016 presidential election not only provided context to mourn the lack of democratic engagement and interest among young people, but it was accompanied by a number of conversations about how best to prepare young people to be citizens. The National Association of Scholars released a report entitled *Making Citizens: How American Universities Teach Civics*. The central argument of the report was that colleges and universities are practicing "new civics," which

> builds on 'service-learning,' which is an effort to divert students from the classroom to vocational training as community activists. By rebranding itself as 'civic engagement,' service learning succeeded in capturing nearly all the funding that formerly supported the old civics. In practice this means that instead of teaching college students the foundations of law, liberty, and self-government, colleges teach students how to organize protests, occupy buildings, and stage demonstrations. These are indeed forms of 'civic engagement,' but they are far from being a genuine substitute for learning how to be a full participant in our republic. (Randall, 2017, p. 9)

The report argued that "new civics" ought to be abandoned, and that all public colleges and universities be mandated to provide traditional civics classes that "teach the history, nature, and functions of our institutions of self-government" (Randall, 2017, p. 10).

The "new civics" approach is of course not new at all. In 1916 the American Political Science Association released its report on civics instruction in the United States and characterized the pedagogy of focus on "the local environment—the immediate community in which the child lives and with which he comes in daily contact" (Haines, 1916, p. 6) as the "new civics." The new civics—in 1916!—did not denigrate the importance of knowledge of government:

> Constitutions, statutes, officers and their duties are merely approached from the standpoint of the functions which are being performed by the agents of government in any political unit. The natural steps are, first to raise the question, what methods are devised to protect the health, the life and the property of the community. The answer to these queries will lead, secondly, to the consideration of the functions of local and state officers as well as to the services rendered by the federal government. (Haines, 1916, p. 6)

This quote suggests that advocates of the new civics in 1916 (and 2016) believed that civic interest and civic knowledge arise from participation in local spheres of political life. The National Association of Scholars report's redoubled focus on civic knowledge and critique of civic activity seems ill-targeted.

The criticism is ill-targeted—but not wrong. In fact, in recent years civic knowledge has been at the heart of debates about citizenship. One line of argument (see Crain, 2016 for an introduction) suggests that the broad ignorance of most voters in most democracies may preclude effective governance. That citizens of the United States know little about their country, its history, and its governance is not surprising. There are regular reports that native-born Americans would fail the test of civic knowledge required of foreign-born immigrants seeking to become U.S. citizens (see e.g., Sigillito, 2016). Many American citizens apparently lack even the most basic knowledge of how the federal government works. Sigillito (2016) reports that one-third of Americans cannot name even one of the three branches of the federal government.

Some political theorists have begun to argue that the ignorance of many voters is so deep that it cannot be easily remediated and that ignorant citizens should not be permitted to vote. Brennan (2016) has argued for the merits of an *epistocracy*, which is democracy limited to a subsample of citizens proven to be knowledgeable; an informed citizenry would be able to make judgments that can guide government in directions that are both fair and productive (for a review, see Somin, 2016). It is difficult to imagine popular support for an epistocratic system of governance, and consequently it is not a proposal for government reform. But it does provide a view of civic life in which civic knowledge is of superordinate importance.

An altogether different view of citizenship has been offered by Achen and Bartels (2016). Their review of democratic theory and political science research suggests that voting rarely expresses rational choice and infrequently guides good government or punishes ineffective politicians. Instead, voting is most often a relatively direct expression of a group identity acquired via processes that are largely unconscious and without calculated connections to desires and interests. Civic knowledge is largely superfluous in the political world imagined by Achen and Bartels; it is probably desirable that citizens know more rather than less about the political institutions in their societies, but in the end voting behavior is largely independent of civic knowledge, rendering the latter an ornament of civic development rather than its foundation.

Although the presidential election of 2016 provided focus to critiques of youth participation in political life and to the models of citizenship to be used to guide young people to maturity, these topics have been much discussed in the last several decades. Youth voting rates have been declining for forty years, and the causes for it carefully examined (Wattenberg, 2012). The civic ignorance of young people has been extensively documented and reported, based in part on nationally administered civics tests. Niemi and Junn (1998) looked at national scores of students on a test covering civics, citizenship, and history. They found that students at grades 4, 8, and 12 scored rather poorly, with the majority being "unproficient." Worse, they estimated that civics classes contributed little to students' civics knowledge. This finding coincided with a concern expressed by both conservative and liberal critics of civic education. Whatever schools were doing, students still seemed to lack basic knowledge of how government works, what American democracy is, and the history leading up to the new millennium.

The findings regarding voting and civic knowledge have been addressed by panels of experts convened for the purpose, with reports issued diagnosing the problem and offering solutions. The 2009 Nobelist in economics, Elinor Ostrom, as president of the American Political Science Association (1996–1997), focused on youth and young adult civic participation by initiating a series of seminars in which scholars from many disciplines met to analyze the roots of nonparticipation and possible remedies. Another landmark was *The Civic Mission of Schools* (2003), a document authored by Peter Levine and Cynthia Gibson, which captured the consensus thinking from a series of meetings of scholars, educators, and policy makers. This report gave rise to other initiatives (e.g., Campaign for the Civic Mission of Schools), which kept alive the message that young people's civic instincts need to be energized in and outside of school.

Meanwhile, a number of books and articles were written to emphasize specific issues on what schools could do to enhance civic education (e.g., Levine, 2007, 2013; Hess, 2009; Hess & McAvoy, 2014; Campbell, Levinson, & Hess, 2012; Westheimer, 2015), how local political conditions enable or inhibit civic education (Gimpel, Lay, & Schucknecht, 2003), what young people in the United States and western Europe know and think about democracy (e.g., Flanagan, 2013; Youniss & Levine, 2009), whether the Internet and IT might promote engagement (e.g., Milner, 2010; Hindman, 2009; Neuman, Bimber, & Hindman, 2011), whether and what kinds of service may be gateways to political involvement (Boyte, 2004; Hart, et al., 2007; Pancer, et al., 2007; Youniss & Yates, 1997), what was being done to ensure participation of Hispanic and African American youth (Kirshner, 2015; Kirshner & Ginwright, 2012; Watts & Flanagan, 2007), how youth participation in our country compares with that of youth around the world (Torney-Purta, et al., 2001) and the degree to which youth in other countries were politically engaged (Hooghe, Oser, & Marien, 2016; Reinders, 2012; Stolle & Cruz,

2005), whether and how the "youth deficit" is driven by an economic gap (Levinson, 2014; Zaff, Youniss, & Gibson, 2009), and what government's responsibility ought to be in promoting youth engagement (Sirianni, 2009). At the same time, a number of websites promoting youth engagement arose with a focus on, for instance, mobilizing voters, promoting social justice for laborers, and supporting immigrants on the path to education and citizenship. And importantly, the Pew Charitable Trusts supported the founding of the Center for Information, Research and Civic Learning and Education (CIRCLE) in 2001. Since that date, CIRCLE has been instrumental in linking scholars with common interests, putting information about youth engagement in the public media, and helping to forge evidence-based policy.

Parallel to this work, a number of scholars have looked at the role of higher education in promoting young people's political engagement. For example, Colby, Beaumont, Ehrlich, and Corngold (2007) and Colby, Ehrlich, Beaumont, and Stephens (2003) explored several campuses to determine the variety of programs that concertedly promote active citizenship and the various rationales used to engage students. These questions were considered also more broadly regarding the historical role that higher education should and does play in preparing leaders within our democratic context (Delbanco, 2012).

Although observations of low percentages of youth voting and widespread civic ignorance among teens are reasons for thirty years of interest in youth civic engagement, they do not by themselves constitute a full explanation for the waxing and waning of societal concern in political socialization. We just outlined some of the work that suggests that in the last forty years civic engagement among youth has received much attention in social policy and political science. Earlier in the chapter, we also referred to a 1916 report of the American Political Science Association on promoting in youth an understanding of government. As Schachter (1998) noted, in the first two decades of the 20th century the American Political Science Association took the preparation of young people for citizenship very seriously, as did numerous other organizations.

Few cultural phenomena—the salience of civic education being one—can be explained by single factors. However, the waxing and waning of interest in citizenship education is most likely connected to immigration. We examined this possibility systematically by charting by year the cultural emphasis on civic education, using techniques drawn from computer-aided text analysis. We examined the co-occurrence of words connoting politics and civic engagement ("politics," "political," "vote," "civic," "volunteer") and words suggestive of youth ("teenager," "adolescent," "young adult," "youth") in books published in the United States in the past 120 years, using the word "corpus" collected and made public by Google. This corpus is a rich source for examining cultural change in the United States and has been used for this purpose quite often. The top panel of Figure 1-1 suggests that the co-occurrence (the measure of co-occurrence used here is the Jaccard Similarity Index; details of our approach can be found in Hart & Sulik, 2014) of the words connoting politics and civic engagement increased at the beginning of the 20th century, became less common toward mid-century, and then dramatically increased in likelihood beginning in the late 1960s and early 1970s: this was around the time the country was considering adoption of the 26th Amendment to the Constitution, which extended the right to vote to 18-, 19- and 20-year-olds. The co-occurrence of these two classes of words peaked in the last years of the 20th century and then increased to new highs in the first decade of the 21st century. We interpret the trend illustrated in the top panel of Figure 1-1 as consistent with our claim that interest in youth and politics is as great now—as reflected in books published in the United States—as at any other time in the last 100 years of American history.

The number of immigrants admitted to legal residence in the United States (data from the U.S. Department of Homeland Security, 2011) per 1,000 people in the United States is plotted in the bottom panel of Figure 1-1. The historical trend in immigration parallels to a substantial degree cultural interest in civic education; when immigration is high (e.g., at the beginning of the 20th century and at the end of it) so, too, is the concern with citizenship development.

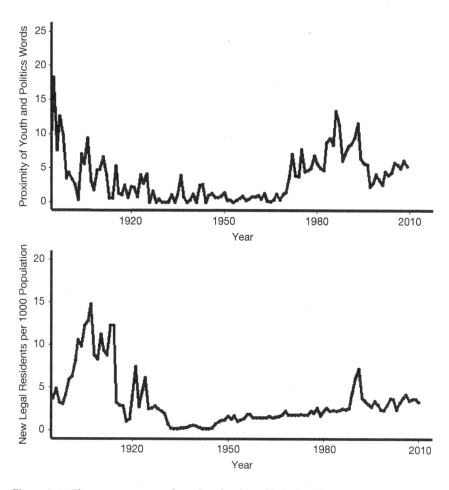

Figure 1-1. The co-occurrence of words in books published in the United States concerning youth and politics as a function of historical time.

High rates of immigration make questions about citizenship relevant: What kind of person ought to be admitted to the United States as a potential citizen? What are the crucial qualities of citizenship that applicants must have? How can we prepare the children of legal immigrants—who, if born in the United States are citizens—to sustain the essential political institutions and traditions? And immigration brings fear as well; there is a natural tendency for people to be vigilant of those whose speech, appearance, and customs are unfamiliar. Recruiting schools to promote cultural assimilation through civic education may be one way that fearful citizens respond to high rates of immigration.

WHAT DOES THIS BOOK OFFER?

We make four arguments, developed in detail in the succeeding chapters.

The first of these is that *youth can be part of the solution to the problems of contemporary American democracy.* Chapter 2 presents a summary of what political scientists say about contemporary politics and the systemic ills that have allowed ideological polarization to stymie the democratic process. In our view, civic education must be located in the political context in which it occurs. One implication—developed in chapter 2 and subsequent chapters—is that citizen participation is a reflection of the political system rather than a consequence of immutable characteristics of citizens.

Typically the perceived political shortcomings of young people are framed as one consequence of coming of age in a flawed political system. This view is of the form that if youth grow up in a society in which effective governance is undermined by political polarization, which is true of the U.S. government in the second decade of the 21st century, then youth become disaffected and ideological as well. But this interpretation overlooks the possibility that youth can transform the system and do not passively internalize it. The remedy for the political ills of the country will not magically appear in some future election courtesy of a better class of leadership: it has to come from the demands and actions of better and more capable citizens (e.g., Boyte, 2004; Levine, 2013). We believe that youth could be one source of this better citizenry that the country needs.

Chapter 3 continues to build the argument that youth can be the type of capable citizens we need. We examine the popular notion of "generation" that attributes psychological-political characteristics to whole cohorts of young people; this is the notion that makes the headline "Democracy Turns Off Millennials" interpretable. We examine the data for generational differences in civic attitudes and behaviors, concluding that the evidence for distinctive, immutable characteristics is weak. We argue that if we want better citizens, then we must supply young people with the opportunities they need. Moreover, we must recognize that within the youth population there are a range of skills and cultural viewpoints, unequal educational opportunities, and varied approaches to life. We review several lines of work demonstrating that contemporary youth, including minority and low-wealth populations, are open to opportunities that help them develop positive and constructive behavior patterns. On reviewing these data, we conclude that cultivating better citizens is not a Quixotic quest but an attainable goal.

Our second broad argument is that *civic development and civic education will not be improved by more of what we are already doing.* For reasons outlined in chapter 4, to prepare the kind of citizens needed to rejuvenate American democracy it will not be sufficient for schools to "do better" or to "emphasize civics." Our review of the literature suggests that the evidence is surprisingly weak that schools succeed in inculcating civic knowledge in students. Moreover, the evidence is also equivocal for any civic developmental benefits from state-mandated community service being a requirement for high school graduation. Perhaps schools could serve as potent forces in civic development, but effective pedagogy oriented by clear notions of citizenship will be required. We need much better research to identify strategies that are demonstrably effective in the classroom for accelerating civic development.

Better techniques are required but so are clearer goals for civic education. Proposing that the goal of civic education ought to be the transfer of knowledge about the country and its institutions into the minds of young people presupposes that the possession of civic knowledge ensures thriving citizenship. It does not. We have already discussed research suggesting that voting may be a consequence of social processes, not the rational calculus matching one's interests and appraisals of the country with candidates. There is considerably more to the kind of citizen that functioning governing needs than the notion of a knowledgeable individual. We use the work of Michael Schudson (1998) and Russell Dalton (2009) to argue for a smarter model of the *good citizen* that goes beyond the "informed voter" to the concerned and active citizen. Although citizen engagement as voters is essential, there is more to democratic citizenship. The core meaning lies in taking collective action—locally, at the civic level, and electorally—for personal and public good.

Improving civic development will require new opportunities for youth to participate in the community and in the electorate. In chapter 5 we propose that civic education be enriched by science-based, civic-oriented, environmental engagement. The state of the environment, humans' role in it, and its future sustainability are problems fitting for the developmental task of arousing youth to commitment and action. We show that the understanding of science insofar as it pertains to local environmental issues is well within young people's capacity. And when this kind of science is taught effectively, young people have used it as a tool to improve their communities' water supply, air quality, safety, and more. We argue further that because environmental sustainability is a shared matter, environmental civics is ideal for advancing the kind of citizenship needed to revitalize our democracy. Entailed here is the proposition that ways of handling environmental issues are not restricted to expert scientists or elected officials but must involve citizens individually and in groups. Environmental civic education is designed to give young citizens the kind of knowledge and depth of interest that qualify them to enter the public discussion of what must be done to reconcile long-term human interests and inexorable environmental processes.

In chapter 6 we explore the benefits of lowering the voting age for municipal elections to age 16. We argue that 16- and 17-year-olds ought to have the right to vote, as they possess the necessary qualities—knowledge of the political system, interest in civic affairs, and a willingness to contribute— that we demand of full citizens of the United States. Enfranchising 16- and 17-year-olds, we argue, is not only the right thing to do, but it will improve the quality of democracy and accelerate the civic development of youth.

Finally, *now is the time to take steps to facilitate civic development.* In chapter 7 we look to the future in which contemporary youth will face a much different world than we know today. We discuss the challenges of economic and racial segregation—the former growing, the latter stubbornly stable in educational systems—for civic development. Some of the traditional institutions for civic development, neighborhood associations and institutions for example, are also weakening. As we maintain throughout this book, youth are responsible to construct their identities, but adults, civil society organizations, and government are obliged to assist them by offering adequate opportunities and resources. If our democracy needs to be invigorated, then we propose to begin helping our youth develop into citizens who care about and are able to meet the challenges of the 21st century.

2

Parties, Voters, and Interest Groups

The Current State of American Politics

I n October 2014, Republican Senator Jeff Flake from Arizona and Senator Martin Heinrich, Democrat from New Mexico, were flown to the South Pacific and dropped off near a small deserted island. They swam to shore and spent one week fending for themselves without contact from the outside world. They wanted to dramatize "the structural dysfunction of the U. S. Senate" and "to demonstrate that a Republican Senator and a Democratic Senator could survive together . . . without retreating to separate red and blue lagoons" (Flake & Heinrich, 2014). They were frustrated with the Senate's inability to pass appropriation bills until the last minute and the minority party's filibustering "every piece of legislation" while the majority party "shut down what was once an open amendment process" (Flake & Heinrich, 2014). They viewed the source of the problem as pressure coming from outside interest groups, cable television, and social media that inflamed voters and instigated distrust between the parties. Because many members of Congress lead commuter lives and tend not to live in Washington, they have few opportunities to get to know one another as friends and neighbors who interact casually at, say, PTA meetings or kids' soccer games. Flake and Heinrich realized that their desert island week was not a solution for the entire Senate. However, they wondered whether their colleagues might at least dine and converse casually together, if only once a month, in order to break the ideological barrier that divides Republicans from Democrats into noncommunicating camps.

Congress is not supposed to act as it has for the past three decades. Elected officials should represent the interest of their constituents with legislative and policy decisions that address local and national issues and serve as a check on the executive and judicial branches. Former Republican Congressman Mickey Edwards judges that little of this is happening today because "private clubs [have] elevated their pursuit of power . . . the principal theme of modern political theater" (2012, p. 18). The two major parties, single-minded interest groups, and voters are mired in ideological competition and focused on winning and losing instead of governing. Edwards pointed out that the Founders worried that "interest-based factions would become permanent factions whose purpose is gaining and retaining political power" (p. xvii). When the winner is "nonstop hyper partisan politics" (p. 31) and the loser becomes the public good, it is time to look outside the system for solutions because change is unlikely to come from within.

Edwards and other observers offer lists of reforms that could result in a systems change. Our goal here is to spell out an additional proposal that begins with the cultivation of a new civic spirit in America's young people. With strategic investment of resources for civic development and institutionalized connections between youth and civil society organizations, a new generation of citizens can be formed, with members who respect one another's differences, care about democratic principles, and seek responsible government for the public's welfare. At present, the ideological polarization that stymies good government is reinforced by a polarized electorate, energized by powerful interest groups that gain from gridlock and legislative drift (Hacker & Pierson, 2010; 2010a). While many Americans hold moderate views on many issues, people who bother to vote, in fact, have become increasingly separated into conservative and liberal extremes (Abramowitz, 2010, 2013; Jacobson, 2012, 2015). If issues regarding immigration status, environmental degradation, widening economic inequality, and inequitable treatment across age groups are to be faced squarely, we will need a new kind of citizen who invigorates America's vast capacities rather than one that takes pleasure in a campaign spectacle every two to four years and then retreats to private pursuits.

THE EVOLUTION OF POLARIZATION AMONG POLITICIANS

There is agreement that many of the problems besetting the federal government can be traced in part to the 1980s when some Republican representatives responded to four decades of Democratic majority rule by rebelling against Congress itself (Edwards, 2012; Jacobson, 2013; Mann & Ornstein, 2006, 2012). These Republican representatives aimed to "destroy the institution in order to save it," and to this end they sought to "so intensify public hatred of Congress that voters would buy into the notion of the need for sweeping change and throw the bums out" (Mann & Ornstein, 2012, p. 33).

The movement to bring government to its knees was also advanced by interest groups who sought to lower taxes and turn back regulations in order to spur economic growth (Hacker & Pierson, 2010, 2010a). These interest groups were helped by President Reagan who called government in Washington "the problem" that was holding back growth as well as impinging on individual freedom. Some business and financial interests capitalized on this perspective by calling for lower taxes and reduced regulations. They mounted a vigorous lobbying effort that brought about a new era of money's influence on both major political parties in Congress (Hacker & Pierson, 2010a, pp. 175–179; Mann & Ornstein, 2012, p. 33ff, 52ff).

The attack on government has been successful. According to recent survey findings, only 30% of the American public "trusts the government in Washington to do what is right" most or all of the time. This figure contrasts with 73% in 1958. Additionally, 77% of non-college-educated Americans, a majority of the population, believe that "people like me don't have a say in what government does." Before the 1970s, lack of efficacy was expressed by only 30% of non-college-educated respondents. And approval ratings of Congress have dropped from a majority of Americans in 1988 to a low of 26% in 2008 (American National Election Studies, 2010; Pew Research Center, 2015). Veteran political observers Haynes Johnson and David Broder characterized the new congressional functioning as: "[No longer was] consensus politics being practiced in Washington . . . or even conservative politics as previously understood. This was ideological warfare, a battle to destroy the remnants of the liberal, progressive brand of politics that governed America throughout most of the twentieth century" (cited in Oliver, Lee, and Lipton, 2004, p. 321).

Poole and Rosenthal (2007) have developed a multidimensional model that uses House and Senate votes to give a quantitative estimate of closeness-distance of members of the two parties on several dimensions of political importance. Figure 2-1 displays the polarization of the members of the House of Representatives from each party, derived from their votes on relevant issues (the data are drawn from http://voteview.com/Political_Polarization_2014.htm). Points on the graph start in the late 19th-century Reconstruction era and run to 2011.

Poole and Rosenthal locate the most consistent difference between the parties along a dimension concerning the government's role in the economy, with Republicans favoring little governmental participation and Democrats regarding regulation as essential. Parties were distant in the House through 1920 then came closer together in the Great Depression and through the Second World War. Since the 1960s, however, there has been a steady widening in distance between the parties.

Figure 2-1 depicts the trend that scholars studying Congress identify through observation and interviews. Mann and Ornstein (2006) described the simultaneous "collapse of the center" with the rise of ideological polarization between the parties. They point out that the parties were closer together before the passage of the Civil Rights and Voting Rights Bill in the mid-1960s during Lyndon Johnson's presidency. Previously, closeness on

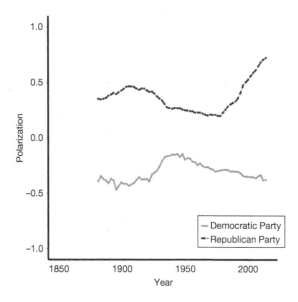

Figure 2-1. Political polarization in the House of Representatives, drawing on analyses conducted by Poole and Rosenthal (2015).

economic issues, for example, occurred mainly because the Democratic Party was a coalition of Northern progressives and Southern conservatives. After the mid-1960s, this Boston-Austin coalition splintered. The Democratic Party retained its progressive-liberal members but lost its more conservative wing to the Republicans. The Republicans absorbed the Southerners who together became a party fostering low taxes, strong defense, and social-religious traditionalism.

There is another way to show the extent of the partisan divide in the House and Senate and its rise over time. The estimate is obtained by the percentage of party members who vote with their caucus when the majority of the other party votes with its caucus (Carney, 2015; *Congressional Quarterly/CQ*, 2014). In the 1970s in the House, Republicans voted with their caucus in 60% of the votes whereas Democrats did so 58% of the time. In the Senate the corresponding percentages were 56% for Republicans and 51% for Democrats. In the period 2010–2014, all of these percentages were elevated. Republican House members voted with their caucus 92% of the time as did 92% of the Democrats voted with their caucus. In the

Senate, during these recent years, 94% each of Republicans and Democrats voted with their caucus.

Such data justify concerns that the serious business of the legislative branch is edging toward dysfunction. Edwards (2012) and Mann and Ornstein (2006, 2012) have asked rhetorically whether Congress today could agree to fund and build an interstate highway system as it did during the Eisenhower presidency or pass civil rights legislation as it did under President Lyndon Johnson. Today that highway system and our physical infrastructure are badly in need of modernization. The point is not that consensus on issues of this magnitude will ever be easily obtained in a country as large and diverse as ours. Rather, we have the technical knowhow and social expertise to address these matters if legislators put reasoned negotiation into practice.

How is it that intelligent and accomplished legislators have fallen into this state of opposition that results in inaction? One answer is the expanded power of our political parties and the interest groups that support them. The dynamics of party discipline help to explain homogeneity within and antagonism across parties (Pearson, 2005). With each new Congress, members caucus by parties to select their leadership. Once selected, leaders are then in position to control committee assignments, appointments to special conferences, transfer to new committees, designation of items that will appear on the legislative calendar, and positions within the party's national structure. The latter may include access to funds that can be used in campaigns such as when leaders allot party money to support vulnerable colleagues for reelection. A combination of rules managed by the majority party, leveraged with money and media exposure, and the election system itself, gives parties at the national level power to seek and demand loyalty and conformity.

Money and allotment of voice in Congress are not the only ways the national party can influence members. After each decade when a census is taken the majority party in most state legislatures exercises the right to redraw the boundaries of electoral districts. With population mobility, this task typically involves re-aligning political districts according to demographic changes. Members of the House of Representatives may be affected when they have to campaign with new constituents who could differ from the electorate that previously voted them in. The majority party in a state then has disciplinary power over members' electoral fate. Also the national party leadership has the additional authority of selecting candidates who want to move from one office to another. As often occurs, a House member may seek to move to the Senate or to shift from a federal office to a governorship. Individuals who step out of line with party leadership risk losing legislative voice and having their career options curtailed.

A closer look at party discipline can be seen through two recent examples of legislation that have historic relevance. One is the Medicare Modernization Act (MMA) of 2003 under President George W. Bush, which was enacted with a majority Republican House and Senate. The other is the Patient Protection and Affordable Care Act (ACA) of 2011, which was passed with President Obama and a majority Democratic House and Senate support. Both acts have a long history, with some scholars tracing the federal government's role in health care to President Theodore Roosevelt at the start of the 20th century. However, it was in 1965, when Lyndon Johnson was president, that the government's involvement in health care began to shift with the passage of Medicare legislation. Since then, relevant issues regarding the government's role in health care, private and public funding, physician, patient, or government's control of physician and patient prerogatives have been debated thoroughly at dinner tables, in town meetings, and through the public media. It is reasonable to expect that after a full half-century, all sides of the many underlying issues have been expressed so that advocates for the various options are well understood. It follows that key philosophical and economic issues comprise a clear agenda for debate within Congress.

Neither of these two acts was accorded this treatment. Instead, scholars have been stunned by the processes by which they were proposed, revised several times, passed back and forth between the Senate and the House, revised by the executive branch, then re-routed through joint House and Senate Conferences. A week-by-week description of the course required for passage of the Medicare Modernization Act is revealing (Oliver, Lee, & Lipton, 2004). This act is popularly known for closing the "doughnut hole" in prescription drug reimbursement for the elderly and Medicaid participants. It was widely understood that the original Medicare Act needed to be revised to address the costs that would mount with rising prices in the pharmaceutical industry and anticipated inflow of participants from the aging baby boomers. Although President Reagan had proposed a revision to the drug benefits offered by Medicare in 1988, it was defeated with a $3 million campaign by the pharmaceutical industry. A similar failure occurred under President Clinton a decade later. Subsequently, President George W. Bush had little choice but to offer another alternative given the cost crisis lying just ahead.

It is easier to specify the groups with direct interest in MMA than it is to recount the legislative steps needed to reach passage. Constituents included people over age 65, the elderly earning over $150,000 per year, pharmaceutical producers and distributors, pharmacists, physicians, hospitals, private insurers, AARP, and health providers in rural areas. This breadth of interests gave rise to issues that spawned coalitions of advocates and opponents. Correlated groupings took shape within the Senate and House so that within- and between-party differences emerged. Eventually, the several revisions to the bill were melded into a potentially approvable compromise that President Bush could sign. The burden of passage went to House Majority Leader Dennis Hastert, whose task was to convince fiscally conservative members to approve a bill that would burden the government with an estimated $534 billion at a time when the Iraq war was costing $375 billion.

Hastert needed all of the Republican members' votes because Democratic members were presumed not supportive of the revised act. On October 23, 2003, he posted the bill at three o'clock in the morning. According to House rules, members had 15 minutes to record their votes. *Washington Post* reporters wrote that 15 minutes expanded into "sheer political drama." "Between the normally apolitical hours of 3 and 6 on Saturday morning . . . the House voted by the thinnest of margins, to pass a hugely controversial Medicare bill . . . the vote, unprecedented in length [as] House Republican leadership cajoled, berated and armtwisted . . . with bribes and threats." Finally at 5:51 a.m., the needed votes were obtained, and the bill passed 220-215, with no Democratic support.

The process by which this bill achieved passage verifies that extreme partisanship had undermined the legislative branch of government (Mann & Ornstein, 2006). It may seem that the breaking of the 15-minute rule for voting, a rule that went into effect in 1973 with electronic voting, was a small infraction. But breaking that rule was just another sign that Congress had abdicated its role as an independent branch of government by supporting the president's will. Instead of continuing negotiation within Congress to reach an acceptable version of a bill, the majority leadership did the bidding of the executive branch and in the process ceded much of its independent identity.

A parallel narrative, although with different facts and other issues, occurred in the process by which the Patient Protection and Affordable Care Act (ACA or "Obamacare") was turned into law. Cannan (2013) has offered a detailed account of the bill's movement through Congress, and we outline his account here. As with MMA, this bill went through a gamut of legislative procedures as it was revised in various Senate and House committees. The issues and constituent interest groups were much the same as with MMA with the addition of employers who would face new regulations and costs depending on the bill's final terms. Some of the procedures followed standard practices, such as moving the bill to committees for markup (open revisions through committee deliberation) and allowing some amendments through floor debate. But other procedures including private, non-deliberative markup and attaching the act to parts of other bills to avoid debate, were legislative innovations that skirted normal rules.

As with the MMA, collaboration between Congress and the executive branch breached the former's independence and shut out meaningful minority input, diminishing the integrity of Congress. Approval of the act was reached at 9:02 p.m. on March 25, 2010, but as with the MMA, not a single House member of the minority party voted "aye." Cannon (2013) asked whether this complex mixture of tactics will have a bearing on "citizens' understanding of how Congress works" (p. 173). Seven years later as of this writing, there is an answer to Cannon's concern. Republican House members have voted over 60 times to repeal ACA. In

2017 the Republicans won control of the federal government, and polarization seems to be increasing. The Republicans planned a replacement of
the ACA without any input from the Democrats, according to Republican
leader Mitch McConnell (Werner, 2017). Democrats eschewed responsibility for finding a solution or compromise: Senate Democratic leader
Chuck Schumer said this about the Republicans: "It is their obligation to
come up with [a replacement]" (cited in Simending & Arkin, 2017). In
summary, the polarization that prevailed seven years ago when the bill
was passed without a single Republican vote remains in place today when
not a single Democrat voted "yes" when the Republican House passed the
first steps to revise ACA on January 14, 2017. It seems reasonable to ask
whether a more bipartisan approach to the issues might have produced
similar advantages to citizens but without the ambiguity and contentious-
ness that hovers over affordable health care.

CITIZEN POLARIZATION

Are Americans as ideologically divided as their politicians? One argument
is that they are not. Some theorists propose that the typical American
adult is politically moderate in outlook, not especially well informed, and
not deeply committed to one side or the other on major issues. In fact, it
has been suggested that Americans would vote for more moderate office
holders if the parties give them no other choices (Fiorina, et al., 2006).
In part, this perspective arises from results of surveys of the public. On
issues sensitive to ideological orientation such as the legality of the death
penalty, defense spending, and gun control, most adults do not seem to
have extreme stances. Moreover, there is only modest ideological binding
of most Americans' views: for example, a majority of adults are inconsis-
tently "liberal" (or "conservative") across a range of issues (Abramowitz &
Saunders, 2008). Perhaps then the polarization in American politics illustrated in Figure 2-1 is a phenomenon limited to political elites—members
of Congress, party leaders, and lobbyists—not the average American as
described by Fiorina and colleagues (2006).

The American National Election Survey has regularly polled Americans on a variety of items that signal ideological orientation, including self-identification as liberal or conservative, views about government funding for defense (approval signaling conservative ideology), aid to African Americans and for government services, and attitudes about abortion and government health insurance. Following Abramowitz and Saunders (2008), for each item, we identified the response or responses representing a conservative view, and coded that as a 1. Responses to the same items indicating a liberal view were coded as –1. We then calculated the scores and took the absolute value of the sum and used that as the ideological extremity score. An individual who selected the conservative item for all seven items would receive a 7, the same outcome as a person who chose the liberal response for all seven of the items. We calculated the ideological extremity score for those under 30 who had and had not voted in the most recent federal election. Figure 2-2 charts the changes. Although there is considerable fluctuation from measurement to measurement, the overall trend is clear: ideological extremity has been increasing among young Americans.

Figure 2-2 also suggests that polarization is increasing particularly among those who vote. Through the 1970s, polarization among young Americans was low for both voters and non-voters. Since then, the trend is generally toward increasing ideological extremity.

Survey data from a sample of 54,000 American voters in the Cooperative Congressional Election Study also suggest consistent ideological polarization (Jacobson, 2012). Self-defined Democrat and Republican voters provided their stances on major issues including whether the 2004 Iraq War was a mistake, whether taxes should be cut to reduce the federal deficit, or whether they approved of President Obama's performance. In keeping with the above findings, Democrats' and Republicans' responses divided into extreme opposite categories. For example, only 8% of the Democratic voters vs. 69% of the Republican voters believed that the Iraq War was not a mistake. Sixty-eight percent of the Democrats vs. 12% of the Republicans wanted stricter gun laws. Twenty percent of the Democrats vs. 68% of the Republicans favored a Constitutional amendment to ban gay marriage.

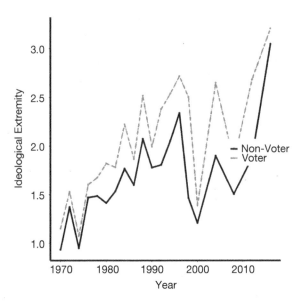

Figure 2-2. Ideological extremity among Americans, measured using items from the
National Election Study, as a function of historical time and voting status.

And, whereas 87% of the Democratic voters approved of President Obama's
performance, only 20% of the Republican voters did.

Jacobson (2013) offered further corroboration of survey findings
with data on the ideological divide from voters as they exited the polls.
From 1972 through 2012, self-proclaimed Democrats voted increasingly
for liberal candidates whereas Republicans voted decreasingly for liberal candidates. It is important to notice that in 1972 nearly 40% of the
Republican voters cast their ballot for liberals and that only about 60% of
the Democratic voters cast ballots for liberals. The latter statistic compares
tellingly with votes in 2012 when nearly 90% of the Democratic voters
supported liberal candidates.

These findings make a compelling case that Americans who take interest
in politics and actually bother to vote, tend toward liberal and conservative ideological poles. They are consistent in their respective philosophical
stances, and they tend to support candidates who agree with their respective views. However moderate the hypothetical average American may be,
people who vote are more ideological, and in Jacobson's judgment, their

polarization "provides a foundation for the partisan polarization observed in Congress" (Jacobson, 2012, p. 1620).

The results from the 2016 presidential election provide further evidence of polarization. Phillips (2016) reviewed the evidence for straight-ticket voting, in which each vote on a ballot cast by a voter is for candidates of the same party. In 2016 in every state in which a Republican senator won election, the Republican candidate for president (Trump) earned the most votes. The same pattern was observed for Democrats. Phillips reports that this is the first time in a century that this high level of evidence for straight-ticket voting has been observed.

Polarization is also increasing regionally. Caughey, Dunham, and Warshaw (2016) analyzed survey results from seventy years of polls conducted across the United States in order to assess the ideological consistency of each state's Democrats and Republicans. They found that taken as a whole, the views of Democrats in a state and the aggregate views of Republicans in a state increasingly diverged, paralleling the separation observed between Democrats and Republicans in Congress (Figure 2-1). They also found that regional differences within political parties—say, rural-urban differences among Democrats—were diminishing. Caughey and colleagues argue that the political polarization observed in Congress is just as extreme at the level of states.

POLARIZED POLITICS AND CITIZENS FOSTER INCREASED POLARIZATION

One central goal of political parties is to get their candidates elected to office. To do so, they seek to get their supporters to the polls. Schier (2000) noted already at the turn of the century that mobilization efforts had changed from the textbook model of simply enlarging the vote (see also Rosenstone & Hansen, 1993). As campaign management became more sophisticated and professionalized, strategic targeting of selective voters became the norm. According to Schier, in 2000, there were 300 consulting firms involved in managing campaigns. They followed "the logic of . . . efficiency" rather than expending resources on "broader inclusive messages for the general public" (p. 102). The goal was not to bring out more voters through promoting an inclusive message but to bring to the polls those voters who would likely support particular candidates. The end result is that parties seek to mobilize their supporters through messaging that is targeted toward them. No surprise, then, that 21st-century voters—who are more polarized than nonvoters—elicit from political parties advertising that appeals to extremes.

THE STRUCTURAL GLUE: MONEY MATTERS

So far we have looked at extreme partisanship and voter bias as co-equal partners in a system that fosters ideological obstinacy and stymies reasoned deliberation. The main dimension of opposition centers on the government's proper role in the economy. This ideological battle is perpetuated through a succession of issues that involve health care, national security, taxation, environmental protection, public education, and financial regulations. Instead of having these matters discussed openly with arguments being transparently dealt with, citizens are treated to strategic talking points and counterpunches that are designed to persuade rather than illuminate or educate. The tit-for-tat fight leads to inevitable stalemate in which the status quo is maintained while reform and progress are held back. Manipulation of traditional rules of Congress, use of the filibuster, and threats to bring government to a halt add only antagonism to philosophical differences.

Why is this state of affairs so stable and hard to change? One possibility may be that money is associated with power (Bartels, 2009; Hacker & Pierson, 2010; Gilens, 2011). Economic interest groups have shaped government policy so as to produce large gaps in income distribution throughout the population. At the same time, these policies have perpetuated and widened the wealth gap. The dynamics start with a growing divide in wealth so that in recent decades individuals at the top have continued accruing wealth while people in middle and lower income groups have either stood still or lost income. This growing inequality presents problems to daily living with serious psychological and social consequences (Wilkinson & Pickett, 2010), bringing into question the practical meaning of democracy.

Economic inequality is not simply a "talking point" or the figment of the idealist's imagination. Thomas Piketty and Emmanuel Saez (2003; Piketty, 2013) have tracked income over long periods of time using tax return data. They show that after 1980 and especially after 2000, individuals in the top 10% of income gained much more than people in lower deciles. Whereas in 1980 the top 10% claimed about 30% of all income, after 2000 their share increased to nearly 50%. They find also that the top 1% have nearly doubled their share of all income during the same period from about 12% to about 23%. Turning from income to an estimate of total wealth, they find that in 2010 the top 10% has about 65% of all wealth and the top 1% has about 33%. They attribute this growth relative to the stagnation at lower brackets to two trends. After about 1980 the growth in the rate of return on capital exceeded the overall rate of economic growth. Consequently, individuals with capital to invest gained while people economically dependent on growth in wages did not.

A compelling case can be made that advantages to individuals with capital to invest did not just happen but emerged with the assistance of government policy regarding classification of income and taxation rules (Hacker & Pierson, 2010). Their narrative connects politics with economics as both evolved from the 1970s through the first decade of the 21st century. In summary, the spirit of reform in the 1960s and 1970s gave rise to public interest groups that lobbied government successfully to use regulatory power for improvement of workplace safety, environmental preservation, consumer protection, and individual rights. Regulatory actions had direct impact on for-profit corporations and awakened them to the value of participating vigorously in future policy decisions. They immediately established public affairs offices in Washington and hired lobbyists to represent them in Congress. As a consequence, the number of public affairs offices in Washington increased from 100 in 1968 to 500 in 1978. Simultaneously, the number of firms with registered lobbyists rose from

175 in 1971 to 1,200 in 1980. These increases did not stop in 1980; in 2013 there were an estimated 12,281 registered lobbyists who expend about $3.2 billion annually (Fang, 2014; LaPira & Thomas, 2014; opensecrets, 2015; lobby database, 2016). These estimates may be low because a great deal of current lobbying occurs outside of formal registries, and it is possible that double the dollar amount is actually spent per year. For instance, executives of large corporations have access to government officials and so have direct communication without going through the medium of paid lobbyists (e.g., Page, Bartels, & Seawright, 2013).

Baumgartner and colleagues (2009) argued that lobbying generates more lobbying. For most important policy decisions, three or four interested parties might be involved, and various alliances might be formed to address any matter at hand. This was surely the case with the Medicare Modernization Act and the Affordable Care Act, in which the pharmaceutical lobby (PhRMA), the American Medical Association, the American Association of Retired Persons, hospitals, nurses, private insurers, and more took stands in the making of policy. The involvement of one group advocating for its interest, say, PhRMA, was shared with other groups, such as insurers, that additionally had their own interests (which, in turn, may have been at odds with, say, consumer protection groups). Baumgartner and colleagues observe that not all or even most policy decisions elicit open and obvious competition. This is especially the case when change is proposed for a standing policy. In many such instances, the process will draw out proponents on many sides, and the likely outcome is retention of the status quo.

Hacker and Pierson add another dimension, called *drift*, to this portrait. Once a policy is established, with time it will tend to be left alone unless a strong force is aroused to change it. They argue that drift has actually occurred since deregulations were enacted and special laws were passed to benefit powerful groups from the business and financial sectors. They cite a tax provision that designates income for hedge managers as capital gains, which are taxed at rates well below regular income. This law was enacted when hedge funds were relatively new, unknown, and exotic. Although we have learned much more about these funds, particularly after perilous episodes in the last twenty years, drift has allowed the capital gains provision to persist. To change it would draw new battle lines between the financial industry and government as well as bring in public interest groups. Moreover, to overturn this tax benefit, the Senate would have to confront the impediment of the filibuster, which has become a common tool used to block legislative change. Hacker and Pierson state that this tactic has been used over 1,100 times between 1969 and 2009, adding to gridlock while revealing the power of inaction.

What further deters reform is the financial power of public affair offices and lobbying forms that have opened new avenues for money to become entangled with government officials. Much has been written about the flow of money and presumed influence in political campaigns. The fear is that wealthy individuals and interest groups can use money to control selection of candidates for public office and thus tilt the playing field in their desired direction. Recent court rulings have heightened this concern, as previous limits on political donations have been removed to the advantage of wealthy contributors (e.g., the contentious *Citizens United* [2010] decision by the U.S. Supreme Court). Analyses of campaign spending by the Federal Election Commission demonstrate the phenomenon clearly. In the 2012 election, 61 Super PACs spent $4.7 million each, matching the $285 million in grassroots contributions from 1,425,500 small donors. A sharper focus on the issue is had by recognizing that of the Super PAC total, 132 donors contributed at least $1 million. Further, a small total of 1,315 individual donors contributed $100,000 or more. According to Richard Hasen of *Slate* (2014), the unevenness in campaign contributions was exacerbated after the Supreme Court's *Citizens United* ruling as nearly $300 million in donations to recent campaigns cannot be traced to specific sources. Called "dark money," this amount comprised 23% of all PAC donations. The danger, of course, is that fewer than 1,400 individuals, many of them anonymous, in a nation of 300,000 million citizens may have a disproportionate influence on elected officials who construct national policy (see also Olsen-Phillips, et al., 2015, on political donations of the top 1%).

Connections between lobbying by interest groups and influence on policy have another dimension that is not always apparent. In what is called the *revolving door* problem, elected officials and members of their staff may make policy decisions with the promise of future employment as a distorting inducement. Several Senators including former majority leaders, Trent Lott (Republican) and Tom Daschle (Democrat), have moved smoothly from legislative posts to public affairs offices and lobbying firms. Mann and Ornstein note tellingly that the switch from elected official or staff member to lobby status comes with a significant increase in income. For example, Democrat Senator Chris Dodd left his elected office to become chief lobbyist for the film industry that raised his annual salary to $3.3 million whereas former Representative Newt Gingrich, a Republican, earned $1.7 million as a consulting historian to Freddie Mac. One can imagine the kind of influence a lobbying firm may have when it hints at a high-paying job for a staff member who is writing legislation (Fang, 2014). In a sample randomly drawn from 31,976 registered lobbyists, LaPira and Thomas (2014) found that 44% had previously held federal jobs. Obviously, hints of future employment with substantial increases in salary are more than an imaginary problem.

How serious are the questions of who governs and how are policy decisions made? Martin Gilens (2011) and Gilens and Page (2014) provide a set of quantitative data that support concern about the role of money in politics. They reviewed 1,779 instances when policy preferences were assessed in nationally representative surveys of Americans between 1981 and 2002. Policy matters ranged from taxation and international trade rules, to abortion and prayer in school. They looked at citizens' policy preferences according to three economic groupings: poor Americans at the 10th decile of income, average Americans at the 50th decile of income, and elite Americans at the 90th decile or higher. They also obtained preferences of interest groups from the economic-business sector. As with the Baumgartner and colleagues' study, influence was measured by comparing preferences to whether or not a policy was changed within a four-year period.

First, it was found that median and elite Americans often held similar views on policy issues. But when these two groups had different preferences, those held by elite citizens prevailed over those held by average citizens. Second, elite citizens and interest groups tended to have similar preferences for policies, and their preferences coincided with policy enactment. For instance, when support for policy was high (four of five in favor) in the elite, their preference was turned into policy change 45% of the time. When elites' preference was low (one in five in favor), policy was enacted only 18% of the time. These results were mirrored for interest groups. When preference was high, policy was enacted 47% of the time. When preference was low, policy was enacted only 16% of the time. Gilens and Page concluded that "economic elites and organized groups representing business interests have substantial independent impacts on U. S. government policy while . . . average citizens have little or no independent influence" (p. 565).

The above findings do not prove causality, but they verify the narrative that money has come to play a powerful role in government policy. In a further study, a select sample of 104 wealthy Americans in the top 10% of income, some within the top 1%, were interviewed about their political views and behavior (Page, Bartels, & Seawright, 2013). Ninety-nine percent said they had voted in the 2008 presidential election, 84% paid attention to politics, while 68% made political contributions (21% helped "bundle" contributions) of an average of $4,633. The median individual claimed to talk about politics five days a week. About half of the sample had contacted a political official, 40% their senator, and 37% their representative. Forty-four percent said that they contacted officials on economic issues that pertained to their own economic interests. These data place connections between wealth and government policy in a fresh context insofar as they reveal a kind of lobbying that would be less common in non-wealthy citizens. When asked about policies regarding spending priorities, this wealthy sample differed from less wealthy Americans on several issues. They gave higher priority to scientific research and lower priority to environmental protection, homeland security, and health care. These items are but a sample of issues that differentiate the views of this sample of extremely wealthy from average Americans on national surveys. They indicate that this group not only has access to policymakers but that these individuals are focused on issues that differ from those of importance to average Americans.

There is parallel evidence that wealth, or income inequality, has implications for influence on government policy (Baumgartner, et al., 2009). They identified policy development on 98 issues considered by the 106th and 107th Congresses under Presidents Clinton and Bush, respectively. Policies pertained to health, the environment, transportation, banking and finance, defense, science and technology, foreign trade, and energy. Overall, four years after policy change was introduced, 58 of the policies remained as they were, 13 changed modestly, and 27 changed significantly. After identifying the groups that sought change, researchers asked whether it was true that the wealthier advocates won more times than they lost. The answer was that they won mainly when they had high-level government allies on their side. It was not clear how they achieved this collaboration but the fact is that advocates utilized the lobbying system and that on major issues the "lobbying community" held different views than typical Americans (as known through Gallup and other polls). The issues with the most disparity involved taxes and banking, the environment, and energy (e.g., Drutman, 2015).

WINNER TAKE ALL

An overarching coherent view of four decades of change in political practices, in relations between Congress and the executive branch, and in voters' views of governments is offered by Hacker and Pierson (2010). They suggest that the normality of political give-and-take, majority rule, and rules of fair play has turned into a serious business of *winner take all*. Accumulation of wealth by a tiny group at the top of the income scale has taken place while incomes of the majority of Americans have stagnated. This lopsided division did not just happen; it was was abetted by government policies supported by both major political parties. In the course of this evolution, political leaders have come to depend on financial contributions to run their ever more expensive electoral campaigns. At the same time, public affairs offices, lobbyists, and wealthy interest groups have entered directly into the legislative and policy process.

Media commentators may complain about gridlock and polarization, but the winner-take-all system prefers inaction most of the time because drift allows people at the top to maintain their economic advantage. This advantage allows the already wealthy to ensure that the right candidates for office, the right policies, and even the right media messages will help to maintain the status quo.

"Winner take all" could imply that if the money or power were pictured as a pie, those who own the bakery would want to have all or at least 90% of its products. This may seem gluttonous and may intimate negative views of and disdain for the remaining majority of the population. None of the scholars we have reviewed have taken this negative tack. Instead, they view what has happened to politics as a systemic problem with widely shared responsibility. Once the norms were changed, it became difficult for any one element in the system to alter the whole. Each piece fit and reinforced the others. The result of partisanship, polarization, and inaction are correlates of imbalanced incomes, powerful interest groups, and the enmeshment of money with political processes. Winner take all is the dynamic that holds these factors together as a system. And that is why change is unlikely to come from within.

PROMOTING DEVELOPMENT IN THE CONTEXT OF POLARIZATION: GO LOCAL

We opened this chapter with the South Seas adventure of Senators Flake and Heinrich, who lived together for a week on a deserted island to demonstrate the possibility of collaboration among members of different political parties. Their publicity stunt has not transformed American federal politics, which remains immobilized by pervasive ideological polarization for reasons we have just reviewed. The state of politics we have just described may explain why so many young people have been generally turned off and distanced from politics. Polarization rather than negotiation, and favoritism to wealth instead of the common good, are hardly incentives that engage young people's idealism or high purpose.

However, Flake and Heinrich did suggest a solution. Individuals coming together to solve real problems could bridge individual differences and work cooperatively for the public good. We believe that this kind of opportunity will more likely occur at the local rather than the national level. If federal political functioning is crippled by political polarization and ideology, cities and municipalities appear to be thriving. Katz and Bradley (2013, pp. 3-4) write:

> Cities and metropolitan areas are on their own. The cavalry is not coming. Mired in partisan division and rancor, the federal government appears incapable of taking bold action to restructure our economy and grapple with changing demography and rising inequality . . . metros are becoming more ambitious in their design, more assertive in their advocacy, more expansive in their reach and remit.

There is evidence that municipal government more closely tracks the interests of voters than is true at the federal level. Einstein and Kogan (2016) found that policy changes at the city-level reflect to a considerable degree the desires of the full electorate. As already discussed, this is in contrast to legislating at the federal level, which seems decisively influenced by the very rich. Political polarization is also reduced at the municipal level; Ferreira and Gyourko (2009) have found that city policies hardly change at all when a new mayor of a different party than that of the previous mayor takes office. This is likely in part because city government is more focused on solving local problems than on maintaining ideological loyalty and because of relatively homogeneous electorates. Whatever the source, the lowered ideological rancor characteristic of municipal governance makes it a better context for learning how democratic governance can work.

Civic development takes place in and is influenced by political context. In the United States, at the beginning of the 21st century, the poor functioning of the federal government may be one reason more youth are not civically engaged. The ideological polarization of Congress, combined with the influence of lobbyists, undermine everyone's sense that democracy is effective in representing the interests of typical citizens. If this system is to change, it will require participants—elected and appointed government officials—with different values and skills.

The kind of citizen that is needed believes in the possibility of progress through negotiation and compromise; as this chapter makes clear, this kind of citizen is increasingly unlikely to be found in political office in the federal government. As long as federal governance can be characterized as "ideological warfare," participants will see themselves as members of a group—a political party—that might be vanquished.

Civic participation at the local level, where polarization is lessened, can be focused on solving problems to the benefit of all. The local level provides a fertile context for citizen development because it provides opportunities to try on identities as citizens, members of a community, neighbors, and colleagues. This is the context that provides youth with opportunities to learn democratic citizenship firsthand. If the future of our democracy is in the hands of young people, then we need to provide them with the incentives and resources that can foster their engagement and earn their commitment to a way of life. The course that politics has taken since the 1980s may appear bleak. But its future direction can change if we can engage young people in that transformation.

3

Youth and Opportunity

S ocietal interest in civic development arises as much from the perception of deficiencies in young people as it does from the desire
to welcome the next generation of citizens into political life. The
young people of today—the millennials—are viewed as negatively as any
generation in recent American history. The cultural breach between millennials (the generation born between roughly 1981 and 2005, The Council
of Economic Advisors, 2014) and older Americans is perceived as larger
than the generation gap dividing young and old at any point in the previous
40 years in the United States (Taylor & Keeter, 2010). Millennials are judged
to be not only different but deficient. In a national poll, and by substantial
margins, Americans judged that older adults had better moral values, more
respect for others, and have a better work ethic than do young adults of the
millennial generation (Taylor & Keeter, 2010). No wonder interest in civic
development has increased steadily in the 21st century (see Figure 1-1).
Older adults view millennials as lacking qualities—morals, respect for

others—that are fundamental for civil society! It is as if improved civic education is the last opportunity to protect American democracy from a generation unprepared to sustain it.

This chapter explores more fully the notions that millennials lack both civic and occupational commitments. Imagining young people today as defined by a set of deficits elicits societal responses of blame and condemnation: "Why won't Millennials vote?", "Young people today don't know how to work hard," and so on. These kinds of responses are common and are reviewed at some length in the sections that follow. While it is certainly true that a generation of young adults disengaged from their communities and their workplaces would be reason for concern, a more nuanced view of young people suggests that broad characterizations of them might be misleading.

The value of a generational characterization of youth varies to some degree according to the purpose of an analysis. Some social theorists believe that history can be interpreted and the future foretold by understanding the sequence of generations. Winograd and Hais (2011) reviewed theory that refracts American history through the lens of a sequence of generations, each having a unique profile of values and behaviors. As the members of a generation move from childhood into adulthood and gain influence as they age, the values of their generation permeate and transform many facets of culture, from professional sports to popular music (Winograd & Hais, 2011).

Identifying the key features of each generation is therefore important for understanding cultural change. Winograd and Hais (2011) described baby boomers—those born between 1946 and 1964—as idealists, skeptical of the willingness of political institutions to operate in accordance with moral and social values. Members of Generation X (born in the 20 or so years following the baby-boom generation) are imagined to be "individualistic, alienated, risk-taking, entrepreneurial, and pragmatic" (p. 13). According to generational theorists, then, political leadership, legislation, the economy, and social policy all are shaped, in part, by the ascendance and eventual decline in influence of generations each with its own distinctive values.

Although characterizing an entire generation of young people may contribute to an understanding of broad swaths of history, the focus on the traits of people rather than the context in which they were formed promotes a kind of essentialism: older adults vote because they are members of the baby-boom generation and are "idealistic"; members of Generation X do not because they are "individualistic." Members of a generation are endowed with characteristics as a result of being born and growing up in a particular segment of history. Change in social, cultural, and political norms occurs as one generation is displaced by the next. The essentialism implied by a generational view of history leads to some degree of despair about the possibility of effective intervention; given the characteristics of millennials, perhaps it is best to anticipate a future in which for members of this cohort, voting is perennially low, political interest is always muted, and participation in the national economy is half-hearted.

Although there may be value in viewing history through the lens of generational change, it may have as an explanatory cost the explication of social factors that give rise to similarities among members of a cohort and may also blur important differences among members of a generation. We explore this possibility by examining the research on millennials, focusing particularly on their participation in (1) work and preparation for careers, and (2) civic and political life. Both facets of analysis support the conclusion that millennials—and probably every historical cohort of young people—are responsive to the opportunities available to them as they come of age.

WORK AND CAREER PREPARATION

The "dumbfounding paradox." A college education is a life-transforming experience. College graduates, compared to nongraduates, tend to be happier (Diener, Sandvik, Seidlitz, & Diener, 1993) and healthier (Cutler & Lleras-Muney, 2006). One estimate is that college graduates earn a wage premium of nearly $400,000 more than those without degrees over the course of their lifetimes (Porter, 2014), making college one of the best financial investments available to youth with many working years ahead of them. The wage premium of a college education versus a high school diploma has grown dramatically over the last fifty years, increasing from approximately $7,500 for young adult workers in 1965 to $17,5000 in 2013 (Dewan, 2015). A college education can be tremendously valuable to young adults.

Given the many benefits of a college education, it is particularly troublesome that college enrollment among youth from low income families, particularly men, has changed little over the past five decades. Porter (2013) called this a "dumbfounding paradox." Why is it that the increasing financial value of college is not paralleled by increasing college enrollment and graduation rates among youth and adults from low income families?

One view on the apparent disconnection between the increasing value of a college degree and college enrollment and graduation is that many millennials are aware of their deficient work habits and realize that they lack the skills and attitudes necessary to succeed in college. Armed with this knowledge, these young adults pursue futures that do not require college degrees and where success is possible. It is quite rational to opt for jobs that do not pay especially well rather than risk college failure and substantial financial debt.

However, the results of two recent studies suggest that millennials are attuned to the educational opportunities offered to them. Zimmerman (2014) examined the consequences of Florida's minimum high school grade point average (GPA) requirement for admission into public four-year colleges and universities in the state. Zimmerman's study featured a regression discontinuity design. The essence of this design in the context of Zimmerman's work is that high school students whose GPAs are just slightly below the minimum mandated by Florida are largely indistinguishable in academic ability from those marginally above the threshold. The idea, then, is to compare enrollment and graduation rates among those just above and just below the threshold, assuming that these students are generally equal in ability. Zimmerman focused on students at Florida International University, a public university, one that was particularly generous to students in its computation of high school GPA. The consequence was that students just above the GPA threshold for admission into Florida International University would likely have been rejected for admission into most other public universities in the state.

Not surprisingly, Zimmerman found that students just above the minimum GPA threshold were much more likely to be admitted to the university. Surprisingly, however, this group of students—just barely able to meet the GPA threshold, likely to have been rejected for admission by most other schools in the state—graduated at a rate comparable to the average for the entire student body (Zimmerman, 2014). Finally, Zimmerman found that these students, ineligible for admission into most schools in the state, just barely eligible to attend Florida International University, experienced substantial increases in their wages in adulthood as a result of their good fortune in achieving a high school GPA just marginally above the cutoff score.

Goodman, Hurwitz, and Smith (2015) also used a regression discontinuity design in their comparison of outcomes of Georgia students just below and just above the minimum Scholastic Achievement Test (SAT) score required for admission into the state's four-year college and university system. Once again, the assumption is that those students with SAT scores just below the required minimum of 800—imagine a score of 790—are essentially no different in ability for college than those with a score just above it—810. Not surprisingly, Goodman and colleagues found that those students just above the threshold and consequently eligible for regular admission were more likely to enroll in four-year colleges, while those just below the threshold and officially ineligible were more likely to enroll in two-year colleges, which have less stringent standards. Although those students just below the SAT threshold could have earned degrees in two-year colleges and then attended a four-year college, the likelihood of these students earning a degree from a four-year college or university was substantially lower than that of students just above the SAT threshold who began their postsecondary educations in four-year colleges or universities. The benefits of being just above the threshold were particularly salient for students from low income families.

These two studies demonstrate that millennials from low-income families and those who had less successful high school careers, given the opportunity, will enter college and benefit from it. Good fortune put some students slightly above arbitrary cut off scores for GPA (Florida) or the SAT (Georgia) and provided access to college. Millennials applied, were accepted, graduated, and benefitted from college. If the cut scores were lowered slightly, Zimmerman and Goodman would predict that those now above the threshold would similarly seize the opportunity. The sensitivity of millennials to educational opportunity is not a generational trait or characteristic of only Americans. When the student riots in France in the 1960s led the national government to expand by 30% the number of slots available to a cohort of students born in a single year, enrollment increased, the graduation rate was unaffected, and a decade later this birth cohort was earning more money than cohorts just a year younger or a year older (Maurin & McNally, 2008).

These studies all point to the sensitivity of youth to the educational opportunities afforded them by their societies. Is it important for economic and other reasons for a culture to increase the number of young adults who graduate from college? The evidence just reviewed indicates that this can be accomplished at least in part by increasing access to it. By slightly changing relatively arbitrary threshold scores (Florida, Georgia) or the number of slots available in universities (France), it is possible for a society to change the course of adulthood for hundreds of thousands of youth at the cusp of adulthood. Youth grow into the opportunities provided by the prevailing educational institutions.

What about work? Do millennials want to work? Survey research suggests that millennials value leisure substantially more and work considerably less than do members of previous generations (Twenge, Campbell, Hoffman, & Lance, 2010). Twenge and her colleagues also report that millennials find less in work of intrinsic value but are very oriented to the extrinsic rewards—money, recognition, privilege—that can be derived from employment. The Council of Economic Advisors (2014, p. 11) concludes, "In sum, quality of life appears to be a focus of this generation: Millennials value staying close to family and friends, having free time for recreation, and working in creative jobs." Hartman (2014) reviews the research evidence and writes, "In surveys, middle-aged business owners and hiring managers say the new workers [Millennials] lack the attitudes and behaviors needed for job success. They don't have a strong work ethic, these reports say. They're not motivated and don't take the initiative. They're undependable and not committed to their employers. They need constant affirmation and expect rapid advancement." The characteristics of millennials suggest a generation that has little interest in working.

Of course work is a function of the job market as well as of the psychology of individuals. Given the opportunity, millennials want to work. New York City offers youth (ages 14 to 21) jobs through its Summer Youth Employment Program (SYEP). The program focuses on youth from low-income families in the hopes that even modest summer incomes contribute to family welfare. During the years 2005–2008, SYEP received nearly 300,000 applications and was able to offer employment to about half that number, with those receiving job offers randomly selected from the full pool (Gelber, Isen, & Kessler, 2014).

Those receiving jobs from the SYEP can be compared to those who applied but were not offered employment. From this comparison, it is possible to assess the impact of employment for millennials from low income families in New York City. These analyses have been done by Schwartz, Leos-Urbel, and Wiswall (2015), and Gelber and colleagues (Gelber, Isen, & Kessler, 2014), who used administrative data (from the New York City Department of Education, Internal Revenue Service, New York Department of Corrections and Community Supervision, and New York City Department of Health and Mental Hygiene). Not surprisingly, the offer of employment from SYEP resulted in an increase in income for participants for the summer for which they were selected. Most importantly, summer employment had a variety of other benefits.

First, participation in the SYEP program, particularly for several summers, improved school attendance and raises academic achievement (Schwartz, Leos-Urbel, & Wiswall, 2015). Second, SYEP enrollment decreased the likelihood of incarceration. During the summer of participation, those 19 years of age and older were 50% less likely to be incarcerated than those not in the SYEP program; employment quite obviously displaced to a substantial degree criminal activity. SYEP participation seemed to provide some protection against incarceration even outside of the summer employment period, as job recipients were about 10% less likely to have any record of incarceration than were those denied positions (Gelber, Isen, & Kessler, 2014).

Third, and remarkably, SYEP participants were less likely to die (Gelber, Isen, & Kessler, 2014). Those not accepted in SYEP were more likely to die from homicide, suicide, and accidents than were those employed through SYEP. It appears that SYEP steered youth away from dangerous activities.

Similar findings have been reported elsewhere. Heller (2014) studied a summer job program for Chicago youth. The eight-week summer program entailed 15 hours of work per week in public sector jobs, and for some participants there was an additional 10 hours of training in cognitive behavioral therapy. Thirteen months later these youths' lives were followed up on. Heller observed that youth who worked, as opposed to those on the waiting list, had 43% percent fewer arrests for violent crime including assault, robbery, rape, and murder. There was no apparent benefit for the therapy. Although the precise mechanism driving this difference is unclear, the program's positive orientation to public work and focus on one's own behavioral management resembles in form the SYEP program.

CIVIC LIFE

Most central for the purposes of our book are the civic traits and perceived deficits of the millennials. Johnston (2014) reports that

> millennials are branded as disillusioned, and their political actions are still heavily scrutinized. For all of the dissecting of their ideological paradoxes, the world is fascinated to see when the generation branded as "unpredictable" and "apathetic" will decide their votes.

The label of "apathetic" reflects what millennials sometimes report about themselves. Millennials on the whole are less interested in politics than the slightly older members of Generation X and even older baby boomers. In one recent poll (Mitchell, Gottfried, & Matsa, 2015), only one in four millennials claimed that politics was a top-three interest, in contrast to one in three Gen X'ers and nearly one out of every two baby boomers. The same poll found that millennials are also less likely to discuss politics than older generations. Widespread concern about the millennials has resulted in worried articles with titles such as "Political Peril: Why Millennials Don't Vote" (Johnston, 2014), "Why Millennials Don't Vote" (Chilton, 2014), and "Millennial Voters Are Paying Attention—So Why Don't More Vote?" (Seipel, 2014). In chapter 1, we referred to recent research suggesting that millennials worldwide (but particularly in the United States) may value democracy less than older generations (Foa & Mounck, 2016).

Millennials' apparent apathy with regard to the political process is not a reflection of narcissism. Some fans of the millennials have labeled them the "We" Generation and claimed that "few people realize how unique Generation We actually is, and even fewer have recognized the incredible opportunities they have to transform society for the better, both here in the United States and around the world" (Greenberg & Weber, 2008, p. 13). One basis for the claim that millennials are deeply concerned about others and their communities comes from an examination of volunteering. For example, Winograd and Hais (2011, p. 266) wrote that

> approximately 1.3 million more Millennials offered their time without compensation to nonprofit organizations in 2008 than in 2007, providing over a billion hours of volunteer service. This increase among Millennials represented all of that year's gain in volunteerism.

Winograd and Hais (2011, p. 259) also pointed out that among those entering college in the fall of 2009—largely 18- and 19-year-olds—93% reported having volunteered.

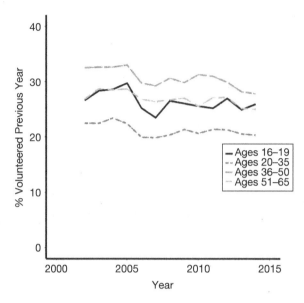

Figure 3-1. Volunteering as a function of age group and year. Data are drawn from the Current Population Survey Volunteer Supplement.

No doubt the millennials make important contributions to public welfare through volunteering. Yet the historical trends in volunteering do not indicate that volunteering is undergoing dramatic generational change. For example, as Figure 3-1 indicates, volunteering rates have been more or less stable over the course of the 21st century. There is little indication in the graph below that teenagers have changed enormously; moreover, throughout the last fifteen years, those between the ages of 35 and 50 have volunteered more often.

An annual, national survey of high school students that stretches back into the 1990s reveals a little more evidence suggestive of an increase in volunteering in high school seniors over the past 25 years, increasing from 23% reporting volunteering at least once a month in 1991 to 37% in 2012. This trend is displayed in Figure 3-2. However, as is evident in the figure, in the same time period there is little change in volunteering rates among eighth graders. If there were important generational changes occurring, with millennials exhibiting civic concern through volunteering, it seems

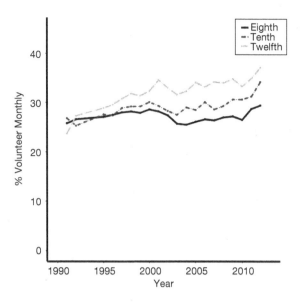

Figure 3-2. Volunteering as a function of grade and historical time. Data are drawn from the Monitoring the Future Survey.

likely that generational effects would be evident through all members of the generation. But there is little evidence of this in Figure 3-2, as there is only a minor increase in volunteering in eighth graders.

How best to explain the increase in volunteering evident among twelfth graders? The lack of historical change in volunteering in eighth graders but systematic increase in volunteering in twelfth graders, and extremely high volunteering rates among entering college freshmen that has drawn the admiration of Winograd and Hais (2011), may reflect new graduation requirements for high school and the expectations of college admissions committees.

In Figure 3-3, we have divided the twelfth graders from the Monitoring the Future survey into those who do and who do not have plans to graduate from college. Those with college aspirations volunteer at much higher rates than those who have no further education plans after high school graduation. Most importantly this gap increases with the passage of historical time; although there was a difference of 10 percentage points between the two groups in 1991, the gap grew to 14 points by 2012. The

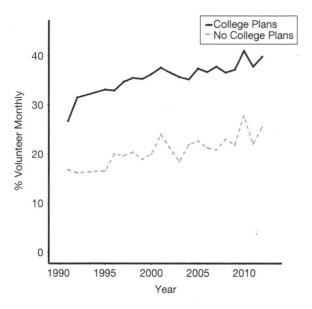

Figure 3-3. Volunteering in adolescence as a function of college aspirations and historical time. Based on data drawn from the Monitoring the Future Survey.

caring and civic-mindedness of interest to Winograd and Hais (2011) seems less a feature of a generation and more the activity of those who are, or seek to be, well educated.

Two inferences flow from the inspection of volunteering trends. The first of these is that the evidence sustains neither the conclusion that millennials are "apathetic" nor the claim that they are "civic-minded." Although there is some evidence for an increase in volunteering among adolescents since the 1990s, there has been little change in this century, and much of it is confined to a small segment—the oldest, best-educated teenagers. Characterizing demographic groups may be useful for marketing firms seeking customers, but generalizations about the civic tendencies of millennials may not provide much insight.

Second, the evidence for subtle historical changes in volunteering as reflective of generational values seems weak. The fact that many youth do service is not in doubt. But its probable origins seem not to come from the youths themselves but rather from outside sources. As previously noted, more and more high schools either require or encourage students to do service (Planty & Regneir, 2004). Similarly, to volunteer or contribute community service has become a valued item on students' credentials for college admission (Friedland & Morimoto, 2005).

Moreover, the research evidence is clear: volunteering is as much a result of being invited into the activity by others, as it is a reflection of personal interest (Bureau of Labor Statistics, 2015). This makes it difficult to attribute the modest increase in volunteering observed in older, well-educated adolescents to generational values such as civic mindedness. To make that judgment we would have to know whether and how service experiences lead to interest in using one's talents for the betterment of others and the community and then how such interest spreads across the youth cohort. Survey research over the past 40 years indicates that the increase in youth volunteering is not accompanied by an increase in the kinds of attitudes and beliefs that would suggest a parallel increase in a concern for the community. Jean Twenge and her colleagues (Twenge, Campbell, & Freeman, 2012) report, for example, that since the 1970s endorsement of values for the self such as "working to correct social and economic problems" and similar others has declined. Given the evidence indicating that entry into volunteering is often the result of a solicitation from another and often occurs in the context of an institution (Bureau of Labor Statistics, 2015), it could be argued that slightly heightened rates of volunteering reflect an increase in invitations to participate proffered by adult leaders of institutions more than it is an indication of generational characteristics of millennials.

Why is it important to understand the roots of young people's stances toward self, society, and politics? Labeling and loose attribution, such as with the millennials, is an impediment to grasping the bases of citizen behaviors we want or those we would like to see altered. Placing individuals into broad demographic categories may be useful for marketing, but it is not useful for understanding how to promote the development of a characteristic or a category, as each characteristic likely has its own history.

Youth vote. Lack of voting by young people is regularly characterized as problematic in close elections. Chapter 1 discussed recent claims (e.g.,

Purtill, 2016) that youth determined the outcome of the 2016 presidential election by failing to vote. One estimate is that about 50% of those eligible voters between 18 and 29 cast ballots in the 2016 presidential election, compared to the 60% of those 30 and older who did so (Nonprofit Vote, 2017). Exit polls suggested that 55% of the youth vote went to Clinton, with 37% awarded to Trump (Richmond, Zinshteyn, & Gross, 2016). Our calculation is that if 60% of youth had voted—the average rate for voters age 30 and over—Clinton's margin of victory in the popular vote would have grown from roughly 3,000,000 to 4,000,000, which in turn might have secured enough electoral votes for her to win the presidency. Because they failed to vote in large numbers, the election results did not reflect young voters' clear preference for Clinton.

The 2000 presidential campaign of Bush vs. Gore elicited a similar condemnation of youth voters. News reports in the days following the election noted that fewer than 40% of the youth who were eligible to vote actually came to the polls on election day, a fact confirmed by later statistical analyses (Levine & Lopez, 2002). This was a historic election in which Gore won the popular vote, while Bush won the electoral college—but only after a ruling by the U.S. Supreme Court. Among youth voters, ages 18 to 29, an estimated 47.6% voted for Gore while 46.2% voted for Bush (Marcelo, et al., 2008). Had slightly more voters turned out in Florida or a few other states, Gore might have won clearly, and the Court would not have intervened. Although the youth vote was closely divided between Bush and Gore, the small youth turnout exposed their relative absence at the polls and raised the question of whether more youth voters would have made a difference.

Watttenberg (2012) has offered an extensive analysis of the youth vote between 1972, the first year that 18-year-olds were entitled to vote in national elections, and 2016. Figure 3-4 depicts the voting patterns for youth and older Americans.

This first year, 1972, was also the high point for youth turnout, with an estimated 49% of eligible youth voting. The percentage then declined election by election until 1992 in the Clinton vs. George H. W. Bush campaign. But in Clinton's second election, vs. Dole in 1996, the youth vote declined

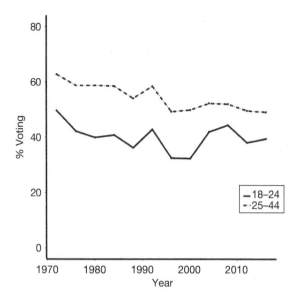

Figure 3-4. Self-reported voting as a function of age group and historical time. Based on data from the National Election Survey.

again. Then the 2000 election resulted in the lowest turnout of all the post-1972 elections. It is noteworthy also that throughout the eight elections, the 18 to 29 voter category had the lowest turnout of any age group.

Wattenberg (2012) attributes the slow decline in youth voting rates to a variety of causes. One of these may be the availability of political information. Wattenberg correlated the decline in voting with findings that fewer young people read newspapers and followed political news in other media. He also noted that whereas in 1972, many youth were still listening to news on the three major television networks while eating dinner with family members, the hegemony of network news had gradually given way to diverse media sources, and families' common news sharing had slowly ebbed away. Since families' open discussion of political events is strongly associated with young people's knowledge of politics, key sources of political socialization that could lead to voting had been undermined during the period in question (McIntosh, Hart, & Youniss, 2007).

Youth voting rates are low in part because political parties do not seek the votes of young adults. Schier (2000) analyzed voter targeting and suggested that with the rise of ideological partisanship, the concept of broad voter mobilization gave way to dedicated efforts by political parties to bring out only voters whose preferences were known through the polls. Neither party wants to encourage more of just any voters and surely not voters who might support the opposition. Both desire to get their partisans to the polls. Shea (2009) found that political parties have few plans to mobilize young voters. He sampled 300 Republican and Democratic county chairpersons to determine whether and how they educated and mobilized youth voters within their parties. A tiny minority said that they expended resources for the youth population. Instead parties focused their resources on voters they believed were likely to appear and favor them at the polls. Mostly these were elderly voters who consistently turn out at the highest rate of any age group. This finding resonates with campaign rhetoric that for the decades in question highlighted issues pertaining to Social Security and Medicare. The result was like a self-fulfilling prophecy. In the past youth did not turn out in large numbers, but the elderly did. Political parties focused their efforts on the elderly and neglected youth. Consequently, in subsequent elections, the turnout disparity between the elderly and youth kept repeating.

The decline in youth voting may have bottomed out in 2000, as illustrated in Figure 3-4, with some signs of increasing interest since then. The 9/11 tragedy gave renewed significance to questions about the strength of our democracy. Survey results taken soon after 9/11 showed that at least some portion of the youth cohort were aroused politically and that many participated in local patriotic rallies and memorials (Metz & Youniss, 2003; Skocpol, 2002). Public discussion of politics rose when the nation chose to mount a military campaign in Iraq to unseat Saddam Hussein. This controversial decision generated rabid pro and con discourse in the media that could not have escaped youth's attention.

There were also concerted efforts by a number of civil society organizations to bring youth back into politics by focusing on their mobilization in the next three presidential elections. Reports show that sophisticated approaches were used explicitly to engage youth (CIRCLE, 2014). Several forms of media, notably the Internet and entertainment outlets, for instance, MTV and Rock the Vote, recruited and reached youth to increase electoral participation (Young Voter, 2007).

Barack Obama and his campaign brought youth to the polls. In Figure 3-4, the youth vote jumps in 2008, the year of the election that put Obama into the White House. In that election, 66% of young voters voted for Obama. Obama's substantial edge in the youth vote over his opponent John McCain is often credited as crucially important in Obama's victory (Levine, 2009).

There are at least three reasons Obama succeeded with young voters. First, Obama's message of hope and change resonated with the idealism of young voters (Levine, 2009). Youth voted for Obama in large members because they valued his message. Second, the Obama campaign reached out to youth. One estimate was that the Obama campaign contacted 16% of youth voters, in comparison to the 3% of youth voters reached by the McCain campaign (Levine, 2009). As we already noted, traditionally polit- ically parties have not sought participation from young people, and the predictable result is that little participation occurs. But Obama's extensive outreach efforts, targeted toward young people, suggest that invitations to action are rewarded by participation. Finally, the Obama campaign made extensive use of the communication tools widely used by young adults, including social media, cell phones, and so on.

To this point, we have focused on voting in presidential elections and by definition elections in presidential years. Voters are typically less likely to vote in municipal elections than in presidential elections, and this is particularly true for young voters. Rates of youth voting are considerably lower in municipal elections. Recent research (cited in Maciag, 2017) by a group headed by Phillip Keisling at Portland State University suggests that in the nation's largest cities voters 65 years old and older are five to seven times more likely to vote than are those under the age of 30. For example, fewer than 3% of those registered to vote between 18 and 34 years of age cast a ballot in a recent mayoral election in Las Vegas, while 33% of those 65 and older did so. While the relative lack of interest in municipal voting among youth is well known, the sources of their apathy are not. There is some focus group research that suggests that youth report that they know little about local issues (Knight Foundation, n.d.), and perhaps the high mobility rate among young voters contributes to a lack of interest in their local communities.

Contributing to the problem, of course, is that because youth vote at low rates, there is little motivation for local politicians to recruit their votes. We have already noted that political parties aim to mobilize those who will support their candidates at the polls, and this means targeted recruitment of ideologically aligned older residents because they disproportionately vote. Keisling reports that the median age of voters in municipal elections in the thirty largest cities is 57! Research on voter mobilization suggests that traditional campaigns employing effective strategies increase voting rates but largely among those blocs of the electorate already inclined to vote. It follows that strong municipal campaigns are likely to exacerbate the gap in voting rates between young and old. Clearly, new strategies are needed to attract younger voters to the ballot booth for municipal elections, a topic to which we return in chapter 6.

CONCLUSION

We believe there is consistent evidence that contemporary youth from all ethnic groups and economic categories are responsive to opportunities that enable them to look forward to healthy and constructive lives. When higher education is accessible and work is possible, youth find their way to these opportunities, benefit from them, and eventually enlarge their contributions to society. Our view echoes policy of the Forum for Youth Investment, which focuses on what youth "need to accomplish to be healthy, productive, and engaged as adolescents and [what] adults [should do] by providing the service, supports and opportunities [youth] need" (Pittman, et al., 2003, p. 15).

What might be the long-term consequences of providing opportunity? The effects of the G.I. Bill, which offered educational, housing, and unemployment benefits to millions of young American veterans of the Second World War are instructive. The benefits of the G.I. Bill were widely available; 80% of American men born in the 1920s served in the military and consequently much of an historical cohort was eligible, and the range of benefits allowed men from all social classes to find support of one sort or another (Mettler & Welch, 2004). Mettler (2002) surveyed nearly 1,000 Second World War veterans, focusing on utilization of G.I. benefits and lifetime participation in civic and political life. Men who drew on the benefits of the G.I. Bill were more active politically over the course of their lives than were men who did not make use of the G.I. Bill benefits (Mettler, 2002). Moreover, Mettler found that heightened civic participation was in part an effort to repay the country for its investment in them through the G.I. Bill. In short, the so-called Greatest Generation, born in the 1920s, veterans of the Second World War, made immense contributions to the civic fabric of the country throughout the 1950s, 1960s, and 1970s. This generation was in part a product of the investments a grateful country made in it via the G.I. Bill.

No cohort of youth is inherently more "we" than "me" in their stances toward society. If we want active citizens who care about democracy and are willing to work for it, then the requisite traits need to be cultivated. As we noted in the last section of this chapter, very little is done in our society to grow young voters or to seek contributions from them. At the very least, the evidence presented in this chapter shows that efforts to instill positive behavior in youth can be effective and that youth are ordinarily responsive to such efforts. Simply put, they are worthy of our concern. The question we pose for the remainder of this book is this: how can we best offer opportunities to deepen participation across the many sectors of youth?

4

Education for Citizenship

n mid-February of 2017, several teachers in Westminster High School, part of the Carroll County, Maryland public school system, were told to remove posters from their bulletin boards. These posters featured stylized photographs of Latina, African American, and Muslim women with attached messages such as "we the people" and "we the resilient" (Chappell, 2017). The posters were intended to highlight respect for racial and ethnic diversity, and indeed the school district acknowledged that the aim of the teachers was to forefront inclusiveness and diversity as important values (Liebelson, 2017). However, because the posters had been carried by those protesting President Donald Trump, the school administration viewed the posters as anti-Trump and ordered the posters taken down. One school administration official compared the posters to the Confederate flag, which itself has no image "of slavery or hatred or oppression, but it's symbolic of that" (Liebelson, 2017), and would be similarly unacceptable in the classroom. A spokesperson for the district indicated that the posters would be acceptable as part of a curriculum discussion that "show[ed] both sides" (Chappell, 2017), without clarifying what the other "side" to posters advocating acceptance and respect for diversity might be.

In late winter of 2003 two teachers and a counselor were suspended from their positions by the Albuquerque Public Schools District for posting materials opposing an invasion of Iraq by the United States, which ultimately did occur in March of that year (American Civil Liberties Union, 2003). The antiwar posters and flyers had been displayed for months before an anonymous complaint was made to the district. The teachers and counselor were told by their supervisors to remove the materials, and upon failure to do so, all three were suspended without pay for two days. The basis for the suspension was the school district's policy that banned the advocacy of a perspective on controversial issues: "The teacher will serve as an impartial moderator and will not attempt, directly or indirectly, to limit or control the opinion of pupils on controversial issues" (cited in American Civil Liberties Union, 2003).

These incidents raise many issues permeating civics education. Surely in winter of 2003 an impending war warranted discussion in civics classes. It is certain that most teachers had an opinion on the matter, as almost no adult in the country was without one (a Gallup poll revealed that 95% of adults were either in favor or opposed to an invasion, [Gallup Poll, 2003]). If the purpose of civics education is to prepare young people for citizenship in democratic societies, one wonders why one or another understanding of citizenship education forecloses the possibility of discussion of important issues. Moreover, it is difficult to understand how discussions in civics classes can advance civic development, if they are mediated by teachers forbidden to express their own opinions or correct the claims of their students. Yet Westminster's and Albuquerque's prohibitions are common in public education in the United States.

In this chapter, we consider the role of schools in fostering civic development in youth. This review helps highlight the limits of formal education as typically practiced in the United States in forming citizens and sharpens our examination of the kinds of citizens we hope to create.

THE CURRENT STATE OF CIVIC EDUCATION

Three views on the process of civic education. Americans have always held tightly to their belief that schools shape students' civic character. As Elchardus and Spruyt (2009, p. 446) pointed out, "The idea that teachers have a tremendous sociopolitical influence on their pupils is widespread." As documented in chapter 1, high rates of immigration into the United States increases concern for the civic assimilation of young people, which translates into demands that public schools devote more efforts toward civics education. For example, at the beginning of the 20th century, schools were charged by lawmakers with the responsibility of preparing the masses of immigrant youth (whose parents were often unfamiliar with how democracy worked) for citizenship (Eastman, 1999). Leading intellectuals of that day such as G. Stanley Hall stated the goal clearly: civic education was confronted with "the great influx of foreigners who needed to be inducted into the very elements of democracy" (cited in Haines, 1916, p. 31).

But even in times of low levels of immigration, schools are seen to be key institutions in preparing the next generation of citizens. In the mid-20th century Franklin Roosevelt stated, "That the schools make worthy citizens is the most important responsibility placed on them" (as quoted in Crittenden & Levine, 2013; see also White House Conference on Children in a Democracy, 1942). The Supreme Court weighed in on the functions of public education in the 1970s in the case of *Wisconsin v. Yoder* (1972), and concluded that Amish youth could not be compelled to attend high school, as the evidence presented at trial indicated that Amish youth had received adequate preparation to be effective citizens through their first eight years of schooling. Faith in the power of education to prepare children for the responsibilities of citizenship remains strong in the 21st century. In a ruling requiring the State of New York to provide more funding to New York City schools, Judge LeGrasse wrote that the state is constitutionally obligated to ensure that schools produce "engaged, capable voter[s]" who have the "intellectual tools to evaluate complex issues, such as campaign finance reform, tax policy, and global warming" (id. at 14, 719 N.Y.S.2d 475).

Although schools are seen as the institutions primarily responsible for inculcating civic character in youth (and have been viewed this way for centuries) there is much less consensus about *how* schools are to transform children into citizens of a democracy. Some educational theorists and school reformers have argued that the processes and structures of classrooms and schools can provide opportunities for students to develop skills necessary for effective participation in democracies. This line of reasoning, broadly construed, includes the work of John Dewey (2004, [1916]), Lawrence Kohlberg (Power, Higgins, & Kohlberg, 1991) and most other advocates of reforming social structures within schools (Haines, 1916, to Edelstein, 2011). Proponents of this view argue that education for democracy requires that the opportunity to practice democracy in school (e.g., disciplinary rules; settling peer disputes) prepares children to be effective adults, while the hierarchical, sometimes autocratic, adult-dominated governance traditional of most American schools blunts the development of citizenship. A more modest proposal—one that does not require transformation of school governance—is that civic development is best fostered in classrooms characterized by robust, respectful discussion of ideas, with full participation of students. Most contemporary arguments for improved civic education argue for the value of the respectful discussion and debate of political ideas, which creates a "democratic climate" in the classroom.

Another view of the effects of the educational experience is that teachers transmit civic values through interactions with students. This is one reason why Americans can become consumed with the seemingly incidental behavior of teachers in classrooms. In one widely publicized case (Egelko, 2007), Deborah Mayer, an Indiana schoolteacher, was fired for expressing her personal political views about the United States' military involvement in the Middle East. Mayer claimed that when one of her "students asked her on the eve of the Iraq war whether she would ever take part in a peace march, the veteran teacher recalls answering, 'I honk for peace.'" (Egelko, 2007). Predictably, given the belief that teachers transmit civic values through such casual comments, some parents complained, and Mayer was dismissed. Courts have consistently decided that school boards can fire teachers who offer their own opinions to their students, based on the presumption that value-laden comments interfere with the official curriculum of the schools (*Mayer v. Monroe County Community School Corporation*, 2007).

The dominant paradigm for civics education, however, emphasizes the acquisition of knowledge of American history and political institutions, with roots that can be traced to the early 19th century in Horace Mann's "common schools" (Crittenden & Levine, 2013). Proponents of this view believe students are prepared for citizenship by acquiring this knowledge while simultaneously acquiring loyalty to the United States. We discussed this view in chapter 1 and noted that some groups (such as the National Association of Scholars) believe that contemporary education has strayed from the goal of transmitting civics knowledge. We also found in chapter 1 that some political theorists view civic knowledge as key in distinguishing those who ought to be permitted to vote from those with too little information to allow them to participate effectively in democratic governance.

There is substantial consensus among adults about what students should learn. State commissions seem to adhere to a general model according to which students ought to learn about government's structure and functions, origins of U.S. government and Constitution, and key moments in American history featuring persons who made major contributions to the nation. In addition, students are expected to learn about citizens' rights and responsibilities embedded in the U.S. Constitution and highlighted by supreme court rulings. Overall, this model seems to be predicated on the concept of cultivating "informed voters" who understand American democracy and what their roles are within it.

Some scholars believe the curriculum is well formed but is too extensive for any student to master (e.g., Levine, 2012). They argue the material mounts as students proceed from the Revolutionary War to the Civil War, from the institution of slavery to the civil rights movement and the Voting Rights Act of 1965, and from the Second World War through the Cold War. The workings of capitalism are covered along with other economic models, the market economy, and the role of government regulation in relationship to the free market. Students are also exposed to some of the nation's founding texts with emphasis placed on the U.S. Constitution and special Supreme Court cases that have resulted in far-reaching outcomes. Up to the 1960s, most high schools offered three courses, one on government, another on civics, or living in community, and third on "problems in democracy" in which students discussed issues currently confronting society. Today, many schools require only one course which combines material about government with expectations of citizenship.

This unwieldy amount of material squeezed into a course or two seems to have come about in part because of polarized politics and a correlated distrust that social studies teachers will present incomplete and unfavorable views of government and the nation's history, resulting in passionate criticisms of common texts to be used in courses on U.S. history and social studies/government (e.g., McKinley, 2010; PBS, 2010). Some critiques focus on specific aspects of the curriculum, for example, the examination of the tension between an open economy and government regulation. There are broader concerns, too; advocates of American exceptionalism sometimes suspect that many social studies teachers emphasize unfortunate incidents such as the interning of Japanese and Italian citizens in the 1940s or our military intervention in Vietnam rather than trumpeting the successes of American history. Consider this criticism by Chester Finn (2003, p. 1), president of the Thomas Fordham Foundation, and former United States Assistant Secretary of Education in the Reagan administration:

> In the field of social studies itself, the lunatics had taken over the asylum. Its leaders were people who had plenty of grand degrees and impressive titles but who possessed no respect for Western civilization; who were inclined to view America's evolution as a problem for humanity rather than mankind's last, best hope; who pooh-poohed history's chronological and factual skeleton as somehow "privileging" elites and white males over the poor and oppressed; who saw the study of geography in terms of despoiling the rain forest rather than locating London or the Mississippi River

on a map; who interpreted "civics" as consisting largely of political activism and "service learning" rather than understanding how laws are made and why it is important to live in a society governed by laws; who feared that serious study of economics might give unfair advantage to capitalism (just as excessive attention to democracy might lead impressionable youngsters to judge it a superior way of organizing society).

Concern for what is taught in civic education has a long history in our country. It may have been stoked by a change in the student population as was noted previously. When students were primarily offspring of established cultural leaders, schools could focus on grounding tomorrow's leaders in the basics of the nation's founding. But the task of educating immigrant youth whose parents were new to democracy, spoke foreign languages, and practiced unfamiliar religions, required a different strategy. Instruction changed from focus on the founding texts to providing experiences with government and how its various functions touched students' lives (Schachter, 1998; Haines, 1916). This shift in focus instituted a battle between advocates for the traditional curriculum and progressives seeking to incorporate youth into American culture and instilling respect for government.

THREE CAUTIONS

The power of formal education to promote the development of citizenship is the foundational belief for the often-heated debate concerning the details of civics instruction. Students are presumed to be profoundly influenced by the practices of schools, the kinds of discussions occurring in class, the opinions of teachers, and the facts that are learned. The belief in the power of teachers, social processes in schools, and facts probably rests on considerable implicit wisdom. However, the research base for the efficacy of formal civics instruction on civic development has some surprising gaps.

Influence of schools and teachers on civic development. Contemporary standards for inferences about the influence of schools and teachers on the academic development of students are substantially higher than they were in the recent past. At one time researchers assumed that students who learned a lot were the beneficiaries of good teachers and good schools. In recent years, however, researchers have become more sensitive to the fact that school districts with many high-achieving students have been selected by affluent, education-focused parents through their decisions about where to live. The result is that school districts with impressive statistics attract well-educated parents who enroll well-prepared children into kindergarten; these high-achieving 5-year-olds receive parental support throughout their school years, and graduate as high-achieving 18-year-olds, who serve as beacons for families who seek the same kind of success for their children. Through this process, districts can obtain high levels of achievement on state and national tests independent of the quality of their teachers and school leaders. The consequence is that the difference in reading and mathematics achievement observed between any two students is largely unrelated to differences in school quality; also, average achievement differences between any two schools is in substantial part predicted by average differences in demographic backgrounds of the students in the schools (Konstantopoulos & Hedges, 2008).

For the same reason, separating the contributions of good teaching to academic success from the effects of family support and student effort is difficult. Some enter in the classroom with the capacities to extract every ounce of educational value; others are oblivious to or dismiss learning opportunities. A classroom in which students attend, participate, and learn may therefore reflect the qualities of the students in it or inspired teaching. It is difficult to know which explanation is right.

Two recent analytic approaches disentangle the effects of teachers and schools from those of students and parents. The first of these makes use of newly available administrative records containing standardized test data for large populations of students. Chetty, Friedman, and Rockoff (2011) used sophisticated statistical techniques and the records for a million students, linked to their classroom teachers, to demonstrate that some teachers were more able than others to facilitate English and mathematics achievement. When these teachers changed schools, the academic success of students in the teachers' new schools improved. Chetty and his colleagues used tax records to demonstrate that those who benefited from good teaching also earned more in adulthood. This line of work sets the standard for the assessment of teaching effectiveness and its importance in shaping the life trajectory.

Another approach is to randomly assign teachers to classes of students, measure the academic growth of students, and relate academic growth to the instructional techniques employed by the teachers. The Gates Foundation's *Measures of Effective Teaching* project used this approach to identify the kinds of teacher qualities and teaching strategies most effective for facilitating growth in language and mathematical skills. The results of this study demonstrated that the elements of effective teaching in language arts and mathematics can be reliably identified and include classroom management skills, lively, cognitively challenging interactions between students and teachers, and thorough preparation for class on the part of teachers. This line of work has contributed to transformations in the preparation and assessment of teachers throughout the United States.

There are no comparable studies for civic education. The kind of work done by Chetty, Friedman, and Rockoff (2011) required access to test scores of hundreds of thousands of students, and, as far as we know, no large school district or state has long administered a standardized measure of civic knowledge to its students. The consequence is that the compelling evidence (provided by Chetty, Friedman, and Rockoff) for the long-term value of effective language arts and mathematics teaching is simply unavailable for civic education. Similarly, there are no large experimental investigations of teacher practices that lead to civic development of the kind conducted in the *Measures of Effective Teaching* project supported by the Gates Foundation. As a consequence, there is no equivalently solid research foundation on which to base the preparation of teachers for effective civics instruction.

It might be argued that while our understanding of the nature and consequences of effective civics education is less complete than it is for language

arts and mathematics, enough is known to be confident that school-based
civics education is effective in one way or another. But even this conclusion lacks much evidence. For example, Niemi and Junn (1998) found that
those who took many civics and related courses in high school knew more
about politics than did those who took fewer courses, but the association of number of courses taken to knowledge was extraordinarily weak.
In fact, the number of civics courses taken and recency of enrollment in
them accounted for only 4% of the variation among students in knowledge
scores. Similarly, Hart, Donnelly, Youniss, and Atkins (2007) found little
relationship between the number of social science (civics, history, etc.)
courses taken in high school and performance on a standardized measure
of civic understanding. They found that the average high school student
enrolled in about three social science classes over the course of four years.
Hart and his colleagues estimated students would have to enroll in seven
additional civics classes to move from the 50th percentile on the measure
of civics knowledge to the 66th percentile. These two studies suggest that
the evidence for the effectiveness of civics education is much weaker than
ordinarily realized. A similar conclusion was reached thirty years earlier
by Langton and Jennings (1968). Based on their study of the relation of
number and type of civics courses taken to political knowledge and civic
attitudes, they concluded that "An overview of the results offers strikingly
little support for the impact of the curriculum" (p. 858).

There are reasons to imagine that the impact of civics education, already
difficult to detect, will become even more modest. Fitchett and Heafner
(2010) reviewed national reports on instructional time spent on various
subjects. As test scores on language arts and math have become major criteria for evaluating schools and teachers, time devoted to social studies have
declined significantly. This finding is reinforced by the 2010 AEI study (see
below) insofar as 70% of the teachers believe that emphasis on reading and
math has meant less time devoted to social studies (Duffett, et al., 2010).

A policy question recently addressed through research concerns the
benefits for students of mandating civics education courses or the acquisition of some minimal level of civics knowledge on a standardized examination for high school graduation. Campbell and Niemi (2016) examined

the consequences of changing state regulations requiring coursework and standardized civics examinations on the civic knowledge of students in those states. They were able to compare scores on tests of civic knowledge within a state before and after passage of a standardized test was required for high school graduation. It is particularly notable in this research that Campbell and Niemi's measure of civic knowledge came from the National Assessment of Educational Progress (NAEP) battery, which differed from the standardized tests used by states for high school graduation. This procedure ensured that whatever changes in civic knowledge that resulted from new state regulations were not limited to specific items on the state test, which might occur from "teaching to the test."

Campbell and Niemi (2016) found scant evidence that changes to state requirements concerning civics courses or civics examinations occurring in the mid-2000s had any effect on civic knowledge. They reported evidence that Latino immigrants may have benefited from increased demands of state civics regulations, perhaps because their families were less able to transmit knowledge about the United States than families with longer residence in the country. A reasonable conclusion from this research is that it is unlikely that changes in state regulations concerning civics education will have broad-based, substantial effects on civics knowledge of students.

Classroom climate. Many civics education scholars believe that student participation in informed discussion of contemporary political issues is essential for learning (Hess, 2009; Torney-Purta, et al., 2001). In his review of education and civic development, David Campbell claimed that "woven throughout the research literature on civic curriculum is one consistent conclusion: the most effective civics instruction involves the free and open discussion of current political events within the classroom, or what is often called an open classroom climate" (Campbell, 2006, p. 63). A variety of researchers find an association between students' perceptions of open classroom climate and civic knowledge, attitudes, and skills (see, e.g., Persson, 2015).

"Open classroom climate" connotes a characteristic of classroom functioning. We would expect that observers could identify some classrooms as having this quality and others as lacking it. Moreover, given the consensus for the importance of open classroom climate, we would hope that teachers would lead students in their classes toward informed, open discussion. Each of these—identifying such classrooms and preparing teachers to create the conditions for open discussion—is surprisingly difficult to do.

First, it turns out to be a challenge to distinguish between classes high in open classroom climate from those that lack it. The most common approach to doing so is to solicit judgments from students using questionnaires with items that together measure classroom climate. As the research consensus identified by Campbell suggests, a student who perceives herself to be in an open classroom is likely to be more knowledgeable and more engaged than a student who perceives herself to be in a classroom low in openness. Remarkably, however, students within a classroom do not perceive their shared climate in the same way. Barber and colleagues (Barber, Sweetwood, & King, 2015) analyzed students' judgments of the extent to which their classrooms were characterized by open classroom climates; they found that within classrooms, there was only modest agreement among students about whether their classrooms had this quality. This raises the question of whether it is possible to speak of some classrooms as possessing an open classroom climate while others do not.

Not only do students not agree with each other about the extent to which their classroom climate can be characterized as open, their judgments about classroom climate only modestly resemble those of their teachers. Hooghe and Quintelier (2011) reported that teachers' perceptions of the extent to which their own classrooms possess an open climate matter little in the prediction of students' civic knowledge and attitudes: only the perceptions of students are associated with civic outcomes.

One way to understand the mixed findings is to think of a student's perception of classroom climate as a characteristic of the student as much as it is a quality of the classroom. One student, eager to learn about government, society, and the community arrives in the civics classroom and perceives in class discussions an opportunity to express ideas and learn from others. This student develops over the course of a year. Another student begins the year in the very same class but disaffected and bored; she perceives the comments of her teacher and classmates to be stultifying.

Not surprisingly, this student benefits little from the course. Because the two students differ on entry concerning their interest in civics, their judgments of the class climate are substantially different from each other and from the appraisal of climate made by their teacher.

Classroom climate, then, is like interest in politics. To some extent open climate and political interest are consequences of context. Some teachers may be especially effective in facilitating effective discussion, just as some political candidates elicit considerable interest. But some students are prone to perceive openness in classroom discussion regardless of the teacher's actions, just as some adults closely follow uninteresting electoral campaigns. One consequence of this interpretation is that it helps explain the variability of classroom climate from year to year in classes taught by the same teacher (Hill & Chin, 2014). Each year's students enter with different propensities to perceive classroom interactions as open and informative; teachers' instructional styles may then contribute only modestly to perceptions of classroom climate.

There have been a few quasi-experimental studies that provide some evidence that open classroom climate can indeed promote civic development. For example, Feldman and her colleagues (Feldman, Pasek, Romer, & Jamieson, 2007) evaluated the benefits of the supplemental civics program, Student Voices. Students in the program spend class time discussing approaching elections (in the fall semester, the gubernatorial race, in the spring, city council primaries), as well as using the Internet for research and talking with local officials and community leaders. Feldman and colleagues found that students who received this curriculum knew more about state and local government than comparison students who did not; given that the measure of civic knowledge was tailored to the specific curriculum, this finding is perhaps not surprising. The program also seemed to increase political interest. Years later, young adults who had participated in the Student Voices program as high school students were asked whether they had recently voted, and the observed voting rate was similar to that of students who had not been in the program, suggesting no long-term effect of the program on voting (Manning & Edwards, 2014). Another program, We the People, has been identified by Martens and Gainous (2013) as a demonstration that civic knowledge, civic participation, and civic interest can be promoted through modification of the civics curriculum with a focus on promoting informed discussion among students. There are several positive evaluations of the program (Turnbull, Root, Billig, & Jaramillo, 2007). However, by the standards of contemporary educational research, some facets of the evaluation research are of low quality (Manning & Edwards, 2014).

Open classroom climate may be desirable for civic education, but it is difficult to determine when it is present (students agree to only a limited degree with each other and their teacher in their judgments) and is likely as much of a quality of the students as it is a reflection of pedagogical techniques. It is impossible to know, given the available research, the extent to which teachers can change the extent of open classroom climate in their classrooms and difficult to know with much certainty the magnitude of improvement in civic development that would be affected by changes in teacher professional development for open classroom climate.

Values of history and social studies teachers. That liberal teachers undermine students' belief in exceptionalism is a fear that has little justification. Most American teachers share the values of their fellow citizens. A 2010 survey of 1,000 social studies high school teachers commissioned by the American Enterprise Institute, a politically conservative think tank, found that 83% of the teachers believe that the United States is unique and special; 82% believe that students should learn to respect and appreciate the country; 76% believe that social studies classes should instill respect for the U.S. military; and 83% believe it is "absolutely essential" for students to know the protections guaranteed by the Bill of Rights (Duffett, et al., 2010). Contrary to Finn, cited above, and others' suspicions, the evidence indicates that teachers intend to inculcate fundamental civic attitudes of which all can approve.

Moreover, there is surprisingly little evidence to indicate that teachers affect students' values and attitudes to any significant degree. Research on this topic is difficult to do of course. As noted earlier, it is possible that teachers' attitudes and students' values are similar for several reasons. Resemblance between teachers and students may be a result of transmission of values from teachers to students. This is the interpretation typically made by educational researchers and observers. Alternatively, common values of teachers and students may be a consequence of families enrolling their children in schools with teachers who share parental values. Identifying which of these two possibilities is correct is difficult.

One approach is to examine the effects of the *amount* of formal education on liberal attitudes. In the United States, public school teachers are more likely to be Democrats than Republicans (Skandera & Sousa, 2003). College and university professors are even more likely to be liberal, outnumbering conservatives 5–1 (Ingraham, 2016). If teachers are generally liberal and transmit their political attitudes to students, students with more exposure to them—who complete more years of education—ought to become more liberal as a result.

Although it is true that students with more education do have more liberal attitudes than those with less education, this effect is apparently almost entirely due to family influences. Comparisons of siblings who differ in educational attainment find few differences in political orientation (Campbell & Horowitz, 2016; Sieben & De Graaf, 2004). This suggests that families, rather than schools, are most influential in shaping political values.

Conclusion. Surprisingly, by contemporary standards of research, there is scant evidence to indicate that traditional civic education as practiced in schools has much effect on students' civic knowledge, attitudes, and behaviors. We are not the only ones to reach this conclusion. Manning and Edwards (2014, pp. 41–42) reviewed the literature and concluded that "the evidential base for civic education increasing normative political participation is thin, the methodological quality of relevant studies is mixed and so too are the results." Similarly, Geboers and her colleagues (2013, p. 170) concluded their review with the observation that "we cannot be very specific about the effective elements or characteristics of the different types of citizenship education reviewed here—given yet the lack of overwhelming evidence." Even the most promising of pedagogical recommendations for civic education—that is, establishing a classroom climate in which informed discussion of community and political issues is the norm—is more difficult to accomplish than ordinarily realized because it depends mostly on student interests and capacities that they bring into the classroom.

The absence of compelling evidence for the effectiveness of civic education has several implications. One of these is the need for better research; civics instruction would benefit enormously from high-quality research identifying classroom practices that produce learning (Campbell & Niemi, 2016 also pointed to the need for much better research on civics education). A second implication is that the goals for civics education may be in need of revision. Perhaps civics education fails because its aims are (at least partly) mistaken.

CIVICS-IN-ACTION EDUCATION

One promising response to the difficulties of promoting civic development through traditional classroom activities has been to promote active learning of citizenship (Westheimer & Kahne, 2004). In the United States, this kind of approach is most evident in *service-learning* or *community service*. Two elements typically define service learning: sustained volunteer action on behalf of the community combined with reflective discussion of the volunteer experience. Often service learning forms a component or complement to classroom work. Reviews of research on the effects of service learning (this research, too, is deeply flawed) suggests that adolescents generally benefit academically, socially, and civically from participation in service-learning (van Goethem, Hoof, Orobio de Castro, Van Aken, & Hart, 2014). In studies of especially effective service-learning programs (e.g., Youniss & Yates, 1997, Metz & Youniss, 2005), the experience offers thoughtful discussion of important civic issues, the opportunity to contribute to community welfare, connections to community institutions, and a context in which to forge an identity of oneself as a citizen.

The potential of service learning for contributing to civic and social development of students resulted in some substantial changes in educational policy. For example, in the United States, beginning in 1992

Maryland instituted a requirement that all students provide at least 75 hours of community service as a condition of high school graduation. In 1999 the province of Ontario, Canada, mandated that students contribute 40 hours of community service before graduating high school in an explicit attempt to bolster civic engagement among young people (Henderson, Brown, Pancer, & Ellis-Hale, 2007). In both instances, school districts were allowed considerable flexibility in determining how these requirements would be met by students.

Both initiatives have disappointed advocates of service learning. Helms (2013) studied the effects of the Maryland service-learning requirement by making use of historical volunteering data on youth in Maryland collected as part of the Monitoring the Future Study. By comparing patterns of volunteering in Maryland adolescents before and after passage of the state law mandating service-learning for high school students, Helms aimed to characterize the effects of the new policy. Her econometric analyses led Helms to conclude that "I find negative effects of the policy on regular volunteer activity" (p. 306).

Effects of the Ontario initiative were nearly as discouraging. Henderson et al. (2007) surveyed Ontario high school graduates entering college who had and had not been required to fulfill the obligation for 40 hours of community service. The survey included measures of attitudes toward volunteering, political interest, political engagement, and community engagement. Henderson and colleagues found that "mobilization by itself [the required community service] is insufficient to produce effects on subsequent civic engagement" (p. 12). The researchers did find that those who had deep experience with community service—presumably a consequence of other factors besides the provincial law—were more civically engaged as college students than those without such histories, but this latter finding is well-known (Hart, et al., 2007).

Any number of explanations might be offered for the generally disappointing results of these studies. Given that almost all school districts in Maryland lobbied against the imposition of the 75-hour requirement (Helms, 2013), it seems possible that implementation was half-hearted and perhaps poorly funded. Moreover, service itself was not standardized but varied across students and schools rendering the term "service equiv-ocal." Although the Helms (2013) and the Henderson et al. (2007) studies leveraged the timing of policy implementation in order to make causal inferences from survey data, neither research group had ideal data sets with which to work. Helms (2013) drew on the Monitoring the Future survey, which had few questions directly relevant to civic development, while Henderson et al. (2007) inferred policy effects for an entire province from data collected from first year students in one Canadian university. It is possible that if these researchers had more data and bigger samples of participants available, subtle effects of the Maryland and Ontario policy implementations might have been identified.

England instituted countrywide changes in civics education in 2002, as the result of a government-sponsored curriculum reform led by Bernard Crick (Crick, 1998). The aim was to identify steps to reverse a decline in civic participation and interest among English youth. Among the goals of the revised civics curriculum were to increase students' political efficacy, moral awareness, and political literacy with these goals realized in part through "community involvement and service to the community" (1998, p. 12). The guiding idea was "that students should be able to put their citizenship learning into practice and to learn from practice" (Keating & Janmaat, 2016, p. 411). Schools were given consid-erable latitude in how best to accomplish the goals and to implement active learning, although there was an expectation that students would be provided with appropriate classroom instruction and opportunities for participation within the school (e.g., student councils) and in the community (volunteering).

Because schools were granted much autonomy in shaping the cur-riculum, there was no single program to evaluate. Moreover, simultane-ous implementation of the policy in every classroom nationwide makes difficult assessment of causal impacts of the policy. Nonetheless, some researchers have found ways to identify possible effects of the program. Whitely (2012) used survey responses collected from young adults throughout the United Kingdom and compared those from England who had been exposed to the new citizenship curriculum to those without exposure to it as a consequence of growing up within Wales or Scotland. Whitely found advantages on measures of efficacy, political participation, and civic knowledge for students educated in England versus those attending school in Wales or Scotland and attributed these differences to the benefits of England's citizenship education requirement. It is difficult, though, to locate the source of differences between populations drawn from various countries, as so many factors differ between societies. Keating and Janmaat (2016) found that youth who had participated in many of the active learning activities envisioned by the new citizenship education requirements (school government, debate teams, and the like) appeared to be more politically active after graduation than those who did not participate in active learning activities. Unfortunately, the design of the study does not permit strong inferences concerning the role of the new policy in increasing opportunities for this kind of learning.

Although the federal government of the United States has not legislated civic education reform, there have been efforts by public commissions to advance civics through action in American schools. For example, the Civic Mission of Schools Coalition (Levine & Gibson, 2003) advocated for the importance of student participation in communities and politics (Jamieson, 2013). By 2003 the coalition had succeeded in forming working groups in each state and developing a searchable database of best practices; the coalition also played a role in advancing many pieces of legislation through to adoption by states (Jamieson, 2013). These are substantial accomplishments.

Because the results of the efforts of the CMSC varied from state to state, and within states and from district to district there is no policy or program that can be evaluated for effectiveness. What is clear, however, is that the truly remarkable achievements of the CMSC have not shifted dramatically the course of civic development in the United States. As we noted in chapter 3, volunteering among 16- to 19-year-olds is largely unchanged, or perhaps has declined, since 2003. The National Assessment of Educational Progress (NAEP) assessment revealed no change in American eighth-graders' civic knowledge between 1998 and 2006 (http://www.nationsreportcard.gov/hgc_2014/#civics/scores), presumably the period during the effects of the CMSC policy would be most evident and a minor improvement in civics knowledge between 2006 and 2010.

There is much to admire in the efforts to foster civic development through action. Our personal experience is that this kind of approach can be enormously powerful (e.g., Youniss & Yates, 1997). Yet our review indicates that broad reform efforts to integrate practice into civics education have not found easy success.

Perhaps equally discouraging is the lack of compelling evidence for the substantial influence of civics education on civic development. Chapter 3 argued that millennials are responsive to opportunity, and research was reviewed indicating that youth today change behavior in response to subtle alterations in access to higher education and employment. One reason that civic education may fail to elicit change is that it often does not provide genuine opportunity to young people, at least in the sense discussed in chapter 3.

Imagine students in traditional civics classrooms led by teachers prohibited by their employers from both expressing opinions about controversial issues and from evaluating the opinions of their students. Teachers have been disciplined for these "offenses" as we have noted in the chapter, and Jamieson (2013) reviewed work indicating that throughout the United States teachers are consequently reluctant to promote discussion of potentially sensitive topics in the classroom. What kind of opportunity is provided to students in civics classrooms in which meaningful, societal issues cannot be discussed? We hasten to add that some American classrooms are characterized by lively discussions of important issues (Hess, 2009; Hess & McAvoy, 2015) providing for the development of the skills necessary for deliberative democracy. However, even under the most ideal of conditions—and school classrooms in which civics teachers are prohibited from challenging the opinions of their students are clearly not ideal—reflective, constructive discussion of controversial community topics is elusively difficult to achieve (Levine, Fung, & Gastil, 2005).

Oftentimes the activities of service-learning programs also fail as genuine opportunities. It is not always easy to identify community needs that can be ameliorated by a group of 15-year-olds available for one or two hours a week during the school day for several months. Consequently, service-learning may default to activities that do not offer clear opportunities to contribute to community welfare; students may end up collecting trash, filing papers, and so on.

The lack of compelling evidence that schools effect substantial change in students probably reveals as well the nature of civic dispositions. By disposition we mean charactersitics of the individual that persist over time. We already noted earlier in this chapter that teachers do not by themselves determine the quality of class discussion. Students enter into classes with varying degrees of interest in and ability for thoughtful discussion of community issues, and these individual differences play a big role in determining the quality of verbal exchanges and thoughtful discussion. Similarly, students bring to school dispositions for political interest, political efficacy, civic knowledge, and civic participation (Dawes, Settle, Lowen, McGue, & Iacano, 2016, Klemmensen, Hatemi, Hobolt, Skytthe, & Norgaard, 2012).

Consider, for example, political interest, an important quality for civic development. Those high in political interest learn more about their communities and are more likely to be civically engaged (Verba, Schlozman, & Brady, 1995). The origins of political interest are many, including inherent tendencies within the individual, family influence, the political context, and perhaps school. But by early adolescence, individual differences in political interest are remarkably stable. Prior (2010) synthesized the results of a number of longitudinal studies of political interest covering the lifespan and found that individuals experience little change in their political interest over the course of adolescence and adulthood. Those who enter adolescence with little interest in politics are likely to become middle-aged adults without much interest in politics. Producing change in an individual's level of political interest, Prior found, required a powerful impact (e.g., among Germans, the reunification of East and West Germany was such an influence).

Political interest and other civic dispositions are embedded within networks of stable personality traits and interests, family networks, and cultural contexts. Consequently changing civic dispositions and growing them is more difficult than ordinarily imagined. Surely we can learn more about how to better educate students for civic life and become more effective at it. But it is also important to remember that students bring to the educational process profiles of dispositions, interests, and capacities that complicate attempts to inculcate civic virtue.

CITIZENS FOR OUR TIME

No review of education—civic or otherwise—can be complete without consideration of *aims*. What are the goals of civic education? As we have seen in this chapter, much of civic education is targeted at increasing students' knowledge of political institutions and processes. In the United States, this means that students are to learn about the U.S. Constitution, the tripartite organization of the federal government, and so on. The assumption is that a well-prepared, knowledgeable teenager, upon becoming an adult, will participate as a competent voter.

Civic knowledge and voting are important. As we noted earlier in this chapter, the quality of governance in democratic societies depends upon a knowledgeable electorate casting ballots. This view guided the recent push for reform of civic education and American history. A brief scan of the bill introduced in Congress in 2001, the Hubert H. Humphrey Civic Education Enhancement Act, reinforces the point. The bill's justification explicitly mentions the disappointing NAEP test results that "show that three-quarters of the nation's 4th, 8th, and 12th graders are not proficient in civics knowledge and one-third does not even have basic knowledge, making them 'civic illiterates.' " The deficiency theme runs throughout, as the preamble notes that "today's college graduates probably have less civic knowledge than high school graduates of 50 years ago." In short, the bill's authors conclude that we need to improve civic education "so that children can grow up learning what it means to be an American."

But we believe it would be helpful if schools could go beyond thinking of civic education as supplying knowledge so that students could become more informed as voters. Civic knowledge by itself does not ensure effective participation in our democratic institutions. In chapter 2 we described how the most important participants in the federal government—all of them exceptionally knowledgeable about the processes and institutions of the United States—are unable to govern effectively. Surely if civic knowledge alone were sufficient to ensure good citizenship, the federal government would be more effective.

Moreover, the evidence seems to suggest that the formation of policy views among citizens is much less rational and knowledge-based than ordinarily understood. Achen and Bartels (2016) provided a wealth of evidence in support of this view. In one set of analyses, Achen and Bartels examined the effects of the early 1970s Watergate scandal (resulting in the impeachment of President Richard Nixon) on the policy attitudes of Americans. The Watergate episode reflected criminal behavior, not policy disputes; Republican party leader Nixon and his staff sought to secure reelection through illegal spying on the opposition candidates of the Democratic Party. Achen and Bartels measured change on policy issues that could be arrayed on a liberal-conservative dimension before and after the events of the Watergate scandal. They found that American adults' policy views on issues logically unrelated to Watergate, such as government aid to minorities, legal rights for criminal defendants, and similar issues were affected by Watergate—but this effect was evident only in those with scores in the top third on the measure of civic knowledge. The people who were most civically knowledgeable changed their policy views the most as the result of an incident with no genuine connection to these policies! It would seem that civic knowledge does not prepare citizens to be more moderate or thoughtful in their appraisal of public events. Achen and Bartels conclude that

> most residents of democratic countries have little interest in politics and do not follow news of public affairs beyond browsing the headlines. They do not know the details of even salient policy debates, they do not have a firm understanding of what the political parties stand for, and they often vote for parties whose long-standing issue positions are at odds with their own. Mostly, they identify with ethnic, racial, occupational, religious, or other sorts of groups, and

often— whether through group ties or hereditary loyalties— with a political party. (Achen & Bartels, 2016, p. 229)

There are staunch defenders of the value of inculcating civic knowledge in students. Galston's (2001) review of this area found that civic knowledge was associated with voting and other civic behaviors, though the magnitude of the correlation is often modest, and the causal effect of civic knowledge on civic participation is difficult to ascertain. Jaeger, Lyons, and Wolak (2016) studied the effects of political knowledge on policy implementation and found that in states where citizens were knowledgeable about state government, state policies were more likely to reflect ideological preferences of the citizens than in states where citizens knew less about state government. This pattern of findings suggests that knowledge at an aggregate level—for example, the community or the state—may serve some benefits.

Still, two implications are evident from the work just reviewed. The first is that the goal of inculcating civic knowledge as the basis for informed voting probably needs to be reconsidered. Voting appears to be as much a reflection of partisan identification as it is a rational process based on policy and political knowledge.

Second, and implicit in our review of some of the educational efforts is the view of students as genuine members of their communities—not simply placeholders for the voters they can become at age 18. This theme has a long tradition in American scholarship on civic education and was vibrant through the first half of the 20th century and was perhaps best characterized in the writings of Arthur Dunn on community civics (1910) and was emphasized in the Commissions of the American Political Science Association (see Schachter, 1998; Report of the Committee of Five, 1908; Haines, 1916). Students were viewed, not solely as future citizens, but as capable members of their local communities (Johanek, 2012). Harold O. Rugg's writings (e.g., 1929) stand out for viewing civic education as helping young people think about society and their citizens' roles in it. In this perspective, students were not portrayed as incipient adults who would vote in the future but as members of a democratic society capable of real contributions. In the same spirit, Katharine Lenroot, Franklin Roosevelt's appointee to head the Children's Bureau, was able to say at the height of the Great Depression that our society would be judged, not by how it served children but by how it challenged its youth to serve society (Lenroot, 1934, cited in Hanna, 1936). Viewing teenagers as citizens whose contributions to community welfare are welcome allows youth to perceive opportunity—of the kind to which they respond (see chapter 3) and that is often missing in contemporary civics classrooms.

Citizenship evolves both within the individual and the surrounding society. Civic education is necessarily part of a developmental process in which youth are coming to grips with themselves in the context of their society (Levine, 2007; Pancer, 2015; Yates & Youniss, 1999), and the meaning of citizenship has shifted over time. Political sociologist Michael Schudson (Schudson, 1998), outlines four major eras in American political history, each with distinctive emphases on what is meant by the "Good Citizen." He starts with the nation's founding era when democracy was limited to landholders, senate debate was closed to the public, political parties were frowned on, and leaders knew one another personally through interlocking family relationships. Power and authority were particularized; they came from membership in ruling families when citizenship for the rest of society consisted largely in a "politics of assent." As the nation expanded in population and geography, "mass democracy" succeeded people's assent, and parties took the role of organizing views and legitimating authority that was no longer particular and personal (see Lippmann, 1922). In the subsequent age of reform, the private citizens as individuals used calculated reason to decide how to further their interests. Authority now came not from personal name or party persuasion but from expertise. Edging to the present, the fourth era has given rise to the rights-bearing citizen who calls on the authority of ideals or principles and supports them through reason, expertise, interest group consensus, or a combination of them (see Levine, 2007, for additional support with reference to youth).

Political scientist Russell Dalton has elaborated on the idea that concepts of citizenship evolve and are not fixed entities. He uses the historical evolution of notions of citizenship to refract the civic contributions of younger and older Americans. Dalton (2008) statistically analyzed survey data pertaining to features of citizenship and identified two broad dimensions of citizenship understanding. The first of these is a duty-based notion: obeying the law is central to this notion, as are jury duty, military service, and voting. Older Americans particularly value this perspective on citizenship. Salient in younger Americans' views of citizenship, labeled engaged citizenship by Dalton, were norms for direct action such as being active in voluntary groups and being active in politics through actions such as boycotts and signing petitions.

We used survey responses from the 2006 Civic and Political Health Survey (CPHS), which had a nationally representative sample of 2000 youth and adults to characterize age-related participation in the kinds of activities corresponding to Dalton's (2008) dimensions of engaged citizenship, which is most characteristic of young people.

As is evident in Figure 4-1, the changes Dalton sees coming are still in the making and have not yet become the norm for young people (Levine, 2007).

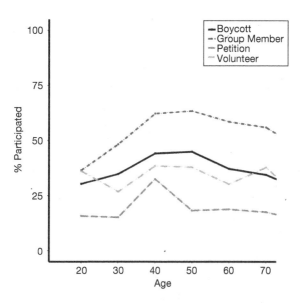

Figure 4-1. Participation in four kinds of political and civic actions as a function of age. Based on data drawn from the 2006 Civic and Political Health Survey.

There are not higher youth participation rates in the kinds of civic action depicted in Figure 4-1 than among middle-aged Americans. And on several of them—boycotts and group membership, for example—young adults participation levels are lower than older adults. Even in engaged citizenship, thought to be particularly characteristic of millennials, young adults seem to lag.

Figure 4-1 indicates that the most common form of engaged participation for youth and adults is membership in a group. It is important to note that the implications of group membership for civic development have evolved over the last 50 years. Skocpol (2003) characterized the kinds of groups to which most Americans belonged in the mid-20th century as "fellowship associations" (p. 4) organized hierarchically in federations (e.g., American Legion, Masons, Women's Christian Temperance Union). Groups were characterized by regular meetings, some degree of shared solidarity among members, opportunities for leadership within the group, and oftentimes engagement with a variety of community issues. For all these reasons, group membership in 1960 typically translated rather directly into civic participation.

By the beginning of the 21st century, however, group membership commonly involved joining organizations advancing specific goals and values, run by professional staffs, and located far away from local communities (Skocpol, 2003). The American Association for the Advancement of Retired Persons (AARP) is one example; to become a member, one pays an annual fee, and in return the AARP lobbies the federal government in favor of legislation on behalf of older Americans. Membership in the AARP does not provide for discussion about important issues, offers little sense of solidarity with neighbors, and has few opportunities for acquiring leadership expertise (the leaders are typically professional staff members) or for engagement in the local community. The same could be said of any of a variety of organizations to which Americans now belong (Karpf, 2012). Group membership at the current time is much less likely to be a motor of civic development than it once was.

CIVIC EDUCATION FOR THE 21ST CENTURY

Our conclusion that promoting development through traditional civics instruction is both much less effective and more poorly understood than ordinarily believed does not culminate in a rejection of school-based civics classes. We suspect that civics and social studies classes can be improved and that these improvements can enhance civic development.

However, our review suggests that laying the foundation for a new generation of citizens, engaged in their communities and prepared with the skills necessary to reinvigorate civic life in America, will require considerably more than exhorting schools to do better. We need to provide real opportunities to youth to exercise their responsibilities as citizens, advance their civic skills, acquire identities as political actors, and to believe that their contributions are essential to the public good. We have argued throughout this chapter that all of these are themes of civics education as well as characteristics of citizenship.

The next two chapters propose two kinds of initiatives that we believe offer the kinds of opportunities that will both engage youth and provide the kinds of experiences that will contribute to the development of citizens who engage fully with civic life.

5

Civic Life Through Environmental Engagement

One lesson of the previous chapter is that advancing civic development is more difficult than ordinarily supposed. Civics education as often practiced in the United States frequently lacks the qualities important for learning, and the predictable consequence is that it is difficult to discern the benefits of classroom instruction. In recent years community service, or service learning, has been proposed as the mechanism through which youth can gain knowledge and skill by providing aid to their communities. Unfortunately, the typical community service activities made available to teenagers as a result of governmental mandates may not connect to youths' roles as citizens. The end result is that state- and province-wide requirements that youth become involved in community service as a complement to traditional civics education yield disappointing results.

The discouraging lack of evidence for the benefits of traditional civics education on the path of civic development also suggests that effective intervention requires time, intensity, and engagement of both youth and communities. We can and must create these opportunities for youth. In this chapter and the next we illustrate what these opportunities will look like.

Our first proposal is to enhance civic education by combining it with environmental education, resulting in *environmental civics*. Schools can work with civil society organizations and government agencies to develop programs that engage students in environmental remediation, steward-ship, and sustainability. Environmental civics has four features: (1) the focus is on the local environment; (2) scientific and local knowledge informs discussion and action; (3) goal-directed activity to improve com-munity life is integral; and (4) collaboration with government agencies and civic organizations is essential.

WHY CIVICS THROUGH SCIENCE-BASED ENVIRONMENTAL EDUCATION?

Environmental degradation is universally crucial for the future of societ-ies. At the dawn of the 21st century, biologist Edward O. Wilson (Wilson, 1993) posed the question: are we humans suicidal? He wondered whether our genetic drives to control the environment and to self-propagate would eventually destroy the world. He reasoned that these drives that are part of our evolved makeup may be "embedded so deeply in our genes as to be unstoppable" (p. 26). According to Wilson the atmosphere is deteriorat-ing chemically and natural ecosystems are being destroyed with unknown and potentially far-reaching negative consequences. Ecosystems of forests, coral reefs, marine waters and fisheries, and the like, thrive on diversity that eventually influences food, water, and air—the basic elements of life.

Wilson (1993) offered the story about lily pods in a pond, noting how tricky it is to know exactly how precipitously environmental degradation can have catastrophic results. If there is one pod that doubles every day for thirty days, then on day 29 the pond is only half full. But on day 30, the pond suddenly reaches its physical limit. Wilson's point is that is that the arrival of "day 30" is unknown with regard to the moment when carbon dioxide in the atmosphere or chemical pollutants in the water become deadly to human life. Wilson argues that "day 30" will arrive unless human societies engage in "ethical reflection" (p. 28) leading to radically different environmental policies.

For Wilson, "scientific and entrepreneurial genius" (p. 28) is not sufficient for this moment in evolutionary history. Scientific understanding is needed but so is "ethical reflection" coupled with democratic politics. White (1967) made a similar argument to scientists. White proposed that science alone cannot provide the solution to our environmental dilemma because it is partly responsible for the problem. Reviewing Western history broadly, White identifies science with the Judeo-Christian proposition that humans, made in God's image, were given mastery over nature and the right to use it to serve their needs. But because they have exercised this right, humans have reached a point that threatens their very existence. For example, by exploiting fossil fuels for industrial production and agricultural expansion, humans have created critical choices for the species. White believes that "more science and more technology are not going to get us out of the present (1967) ecological crisis because eons of Western thought have made humans feel separate from and superior to nature" (p. 1206). White calls for a fundamental revision of how humans think about themselves in relation to the world around them. People cannot begin to address the ecological crisis they are in until they recognize that they are part of "a democracy of all God's creatures" (p. 1206). Reflection should lead to a sense of "humility" that would replace centuries of "arrogance toward nature" (p. 1207). Science generated knowledge that allowed for the exploitation of the environment but the solution to the problems science has created will require moral and political action (see Hallman, 1994; Pope Francis, 2015).

In 1998 Jane Lubchenco published an essay in *Science* titled "Entering the Century of the Environment: A New Social Contract for Science." Like White and Wilson, she described the gigantic accomplishments of science and technology, then she asked whether science is able to resolve the environmental crisis that it helped spawn. Her answer is "no," at least not science as ordinarily understood. In her view, a new social contract is needed, one in which solutions are jointly arrived at by various sectors of society. Science would contribute necessary knowledge and propose solutions but only as a partner with ordinary citizens, for-profit business interests, environmental groups, and government policymakers.

Biologist Heather Reynolds (Reynolds, 2010) provides a synthesis of principles that would inform our proposal for environmental civics. (1) "Human presence is a subset of the larger earth environment": in other words, humans are not at the center of the universe or even the earth, but are partners to plants, other animals, and bio-chemical processes; (2) humans depend for existence, health, and aesthetic pleasure on pure air, a temperate and stable climate, unpolluted water, controlled waste, healthy food, and other resources; and (3) the environment is not something disconnected from humans because the environment provides essential services and in turn, human action necessarily influences what the environment can provide.

The third principle contains an answer to the question of what to do next. For Reynolds, the proper response is to seek *sustainability*. This response combines science with political-civic action because it seeks a balance between meeting current needs and taking account of future generations. Suicidal humans would satisfy current needs without regard for the quality of life for humans in the future. Scientific illiterates would be unable to look to the future because they do not fully comprehend the present condition or how we got here. Sustainers, in contrast, would combine scientific understanding with a willingness to enter into discussion about the future that includes honest appraisal of costs and benefits, trade-offs, and above all, long-term goals for humans as part of (and not distinct from) the larger environment.

Environmental concerns engage and promote democratic skills. It is reasonable to ask if the moral obligation to be concerned about the environment is sufficient to engage youth, and, once engaged, to promote within them the kinds of capacities and values important to renew democracy. The Nobel Prize–winning work of Elinor Ostrom (Ostrom, 2009) proposes that environmental concerns can mobilize people to work together to solve pressing problems concerning natural resources. Ostrom has studied how communities of different kinds approach the *tragedy of the commons*, which refers to the possibility that self-interested actors will plunder common pool (or shared) resources such as forests, fisheries, and grazing lands. As Hardin (1968) concluded, based on one type of rational choice model of humans, it is in some sense reasonable for individuals to draw as much as possible from the common pool before the pool is depleted by others. A traditional response from political scientists to the tragedy of the commons is to suggest that the solution is a strong government that regulates the resources of shared resources.

In a series of investigations, Ostrom (2009, 2014, 2015) found that under some circumstances, members of communities were able to negotiate norms for the use of common pool resources and to elicit compliance with these norms from each other. For example, fish are a type of shared source that draws from communities' efforts to prevent the tragedy of the commons. Those who fish in a particular area and earn their livelihoods from fishing are understandably concerned that others may depress a population of fish to a level that approaches extinction through overfishing. This shared concern for the stability of the population of fish brings community members together to discuss maintaining a healthy population of fish through consensual regulation (e.g., the start and end of the fishing season, the size of fish that may be kept, who can and who cannot fish, and so on). See Wilson, Acheson, Metcalfe, & Kleban, 1994 for a review of practices around the world and Cinner, et al., 2016 for the impact of such agreements for the health of coral reefs. Because the dynamics of fish populations are complex, community self-regulation of fishing is typically an ongoing process requiring regular meetings among interested parties.

Concern for a shared environmental resource such as fish brings individuals together to solve a community problem and thus elicits the thoughtful, data-informed, negotiations that constitute deliberative democracy (Levine, Fung, & Gastil, 2005b): that is, policy formed through public discussion, negotiation, and consensus. Although it is unlikely that deliberative democracy can become the process through which all decisions in a democracy are made—given the powerful pull of partisan identifications

on policy positions (Achen & Bartels, 2016)—the promotion of deliberative democracy and the skills to engage in it are surely desirable outcomes
of communities seeking to regulate a common pool resource. As argued
in chapter 2, it is exactly this kind of negotiation that often seems absent
in the U.S. Congress.

Environmental resource issues bring together people to negotiate but
also to govern their communities and regulate the behavior of their fellow citizens. Deitz, Ostrom, and Stern (2003) identified processes communities use in the self-governance of environmental resources, and they
identify the contextual factors that increase the likely success of community efforts. A shared understanding of the common pool resource, clear
community-membership boundaries, methods for resolving disputes, and
the opportunity for face-to-face interactions may all contribute to successful community self-regulation. It appears, then, that under favorable
circumstances environmental resource issues brings adults together to
govern themselves and by doing so acquiring the skills necessary to allow
for successful democracy. If it works for adults, it can work for youth.

EXAMPLES OF ENVIRONMENTAL CIVICS

We are not alone in seeing the potential of environmental studies to serve
as an entry point for youth into then real world of responsible civic action.
A kind of environmental learning we call *environmental civics* is emerging
across the United States. The flowering of these programs could begin to
build a foundation for the importance of environmental civics in struc-
turing youth civic development. Here we consider examples of successful
programs.

Teacher-initiated programs. On May 9, 2009, Governor Chet Culver of
Iowa signed into law a bill requiring safe disposal of used oil filters, the kind
found on every automobile. Previously oil filters were dumped unthink-
ingly with other waste in landfills, allowing the oil in them to leach into
the ground an array of toxic chemicals that damaged the soil and harmed
water quality. The interesting feature of this bill was the research that

brought the environmental risk of used filters to legislators' attention. The basic work was accomplished by students in West Branch Middle School who were mentored by an innovative teacher, Hector Ibarra, who for years had brought award-winning teams to national science contests. For this project, the students deconstructed used oil filters, tested their chemical make-up, estimated the damage from leaching, and calculated how much oil could be recovered from the treatment process. The students also worked with state conservation agents and university researchers as they presented their case to their local legislator, even as they received push back from lobbyists representing commercial interests (Youniss, 2012).

Another example took place with middle schoolers in Upper Michigan where loss of jobs through de-industrialization led communities to refocus on tourism and the importance of the natural environment. Gallay, et al. (2016) reported on a collaboration among schools, civil society organizations, and government in which students were given hands-on experience alongside community groups in various environmental stewardship tasks such as monitoring streams, protecting local beaches, or conducting water quality tests. The authors reported that students' participation was accompanied by increased sensitivity to environmental issues, awareness of responsible environmental behaviors, and deepened attachment to their community. As in Iowa, schooling with hands on experience helped youth understand that they had a role in improving their communities, showing that "pitching in" was not an added chore but a means to community membership (Rogoff, 2014).

These middle schoolers are not unique but represent thousands of students across the country who are taught to use research to address environmental issues and their policy implications. Various supporters such as the Christopher Columbus Foundation, for-profit businesses such as the Siemens Corporation, and the Federal Environmental Protection Agency, sponsor programs that award scholarship money for winning contestants. A review of environmental education trends and themes (Kudryastev & Krasny, 2012) shows that thousands of female and male students are exposed to serious environmental studies and gives a lie to the belief that science interests only the super-talented 1 percent, that environmental issues are too complex for youth to grasp, that females cannot abide hard sciences, and that civic education consists primarily in the reading of America's texts and absorbing the nation's history. Surely the nation's founding documents and major historical events are important—but no more so than for students to come to grips with their capacity as active citizens to understand the environment and to do something constructive to sustain it.

Community partnership initiated programs. Levine and colleagues (2011) described a 16-year-long project originating from researchers at North Carolina State University in partnership with the city of Jacksonville, North Carolina, Camp Lejeune Marine base, and other communities bordering the estuarine waters of the New River and Wilson Bay. At the start of the project, the aim was to treat the degraded bay and estuarine waters that had been polluted through discharge of wastewater from Jacksonville and eight other communities plus the Marine base. As a result Wilson Bay and the river had been closed to recreational use and commercial fishing causing Jacksonville to lose a key element of its economic base. The initial task was to identify the sources of pollution, diagnose the health of the river, and plot plausible solutions. As this work unfolded, the North Carolina State researchers collaborated with city and state officials on plans and funding approaches for restoration. Early projects included encouragement of oyster farming that would benefit the bay's water through filtration and generate commercial profit; removing over 400 creosote-coated pilings that leached polluting chemicals; and seeding viable plants that would improve river beds and bring back estuarian aquatic species.

This initiative in its various functions included state agencies, city planners, citizen groups, the Marine base, charitable foundations, graduate students from North Carolina State, researchers from two other universities, and students from two local community colleges. This is the structural context into which administrators of high schools and middle schools decided to engage students in environmental civics. In this instance, environmental education (EE) was not about the natural environment in an abstract sense but was focused on the environmental and economic well-being of the local community. Students gave 10,000 hours of participation alongside college students and adults in testing water quality, seeding plants, and monitoring oyster beds and seafood in the estuarine waters. They observed the impact of their work as part of a large partnership in restoring Wilson Bay for recreational and commercial use and the recovery of the surrounding wetlands that became "a living classroom for student exploration and hands-on learning" (p. 125). Students also saw the old wastewater treatment plant repurposed for recreation and community environmental education.

This project also led local schools to intensify the focus on issues of importance to the community. Students documented the ongoing project in classes on photography, journalism, and videography. Physics and math classes began to teach environmental engineering and other classes focused on "negotiation . . . and social skills" (p. 128) that were relevant to the project's progress. Classes also covered the media's role in environmental change and "hands-on environmental work" (p. 128). There is only one reported quantitative measure of impact on the youth who participated. Surveys were sent to 1,191 youth, five years after they took part in the project. Of the 558 young people who responded, 89% were enrolled in or had graduated from college, which for this population was an important outcome of the project. This result was pertinent also to the recovery of Jacksonville's commercial center and its relation to the revival of tourism and commercial fishing.

INSTITUTIONS AND ENVIRONMENTAL CIVICS

Environmental civics builds on existing organizations that serve as links to the public policy. It is worth noting that Hines, et al. (1987) and Bamberg and Moser (2007) did meta-analyses of nearly 200 studies in all, which showed that hands-on experiences, tied to environmental organizations and social-moral concerns, were key factors in generating intentions to improve the environment. These results are all the more impressive because of the breath of environmental education these studies covered: geography, engineering, social psychology, forestry, and political science, among others. It would seem that schools need only open the door to this array of knowledge, awareness, and plans of action, to engage students to the intellectual-moral ferment around them.

Sirianni (2009) had described a decades-long initiative in the Chesapeake Bay area that appears ideal for engaging students. The Chesapeake Bay estuary was once a provider of aquatic recreation and commercial fishing for a several states in the Atlantic Coast region. Pollution from wastewater, farming, and residential construction has degraded the bay at a dire human and economic cost. During recent decades, six states, several commissions, federal agencies, over 500 municipalities, and numerous non-profit organizations have joined in a reclamation effort. As with the Wilson Bay project, the work is long term, but it is ideal for engaging schools and youth by raising standard EE to the level of environmental civics.

The list of government, civic, professional, business, and educational organizations that are focused on environmental issues is too extensive to summarize here. As a whole they constitute an organizational base that schools and students can draw from. They identify issues and provide programs in which youth can participate in meaningful ways. Young people do not have to search for problems or create solutions anew but can build on this array of resources to learn as well as to contribute to society. By entering into well-organized, local, and ongoing efforts, youth can participate alongside other citizens who are doing meaningful public work (Boyte, 2004). This civil society resource helps youth see themselves moving into an established trajectory with a noted past, active present, and hopeful future. Availability of information and modes of programmatic action make environmental civics a practical pursuit. The fact that environmental matters may be central to political prosperity and stability in the 21st century, only adds to its appealing as a citizen-making strategy.

YOUTH AND THE SCIENCE-BASED TRANSFORMATION OF SOCIETY

Recent survey data indicate that young people are clearly aware of the changing climate and believe that human activity is responsible (You.gov.,

2016). Seventy-two percent of people in their 20s or younger believe that human behavior is causative vs. only 35% of people over age 65. This age split holds for conservative- and progressive-leaning youth and likely indicates that young people have picked up on the general consensus on environmental change held by scientists. It may be that youth are more willing to accept new findings of science. Research in different cultures generally finds that youth are more open to new ideas than are older adults (McCrae et al., 2000).

Youthful openness to science can be synthesized with opportunity to result in transformation in community practices. In 1899 a seed merchant from Illinois, W. B. Otwell, initiated an experiment to break through the impediments that kept farmers of the time from taking up innovative practices. He advertised that any boy who sent him a one-cent stamp and self-addressed envelope would receive a packet of new corn seeds sufficient for a one-acre plot. Boys between the ages of 10 and 18 who responded were entered into a contest whose winners would be declared at harvest time when cash prizes would be awarded for amount and quality of yield. Five hundred boys entered the first year. In 1901, 1,500 boys entered. By 1904 Otwell's contest attracted 50,000 entrants with finalists being feted at the Louisiana Expo in St. Louis (Wessel & Wessel, 1982).

When word spread throughout the Midwest, new contests were started in an effort to revitalize rural education. Teachers saw new corn as a means to improve agriculture production and interest youth in sustaining rural life. Youth were viewed as agents of innovation who might influence the older generation. Boys who entered the competitions became members of "Corn Clubs" that quickly spread across the Midwest and in a short time transformed corn production and associated farm output. As fathers saw the abundant yields from the new seeds, fertilization, and soil preparation methods, many of them jumped on board.

In 1908 Corn Clubs became popular in the South through efforts of a USDA agent in Texas, Seaman A. Knapp. He worked mainly with schools to enroll 46,225 boys in Corn Clubs by 1910. Numbers grew to 67,179 boys by 1912. Seaman's goal was "to reach the home through the boys [by having the boys] do one thing well." Seaman's "ideal of education is that of practical sense leadership" (cited in Uricchio, et al., 2013, p. 227). Farmers' adoption of corn was especially important in the South because it allowed diversification beyond single-crop dependence on cotton. Corn could be sold as feed, and that enabled expansion of poultry and cattle farming. In this regard, Corn Clubs helped to transform farming while giving boys a vehicle for "self-expression" within an otherwise tradition-bound agricultural environment (citing Knapp, p. 228).

When female educators in the South learned of Knapp's work, they wondered whether they could do the same for girls. Marie Samuella Cromer in South Carolina and associates in North Carolina, Mississippi, Virginia, and Tennessee, started Tomato Clubs for girls, ages 12 to 18. These educators provided girl contestants with seeds for 1/10- acre plots along with instructions for soil preparation and canning. The first winner in South Carolina, Katie Gunter, produced tomatoes for 512 cans that were sold for a profit of $35.00. In North Carolina, Tomato Clubs caught on quickly so that by 1913, 1,500 girls participated and by 1914, 2,914 girls made an average profit of nearly $40. By 1915, 32,613 North Carolina club members produced over 5 million pounds of tomatoes (Englehardt, 2009). As with the boys, educators sought to weave girls more tightly into their rural environments by giving them meaningful roles as innovators. As a result of Tomato Clubs, family nutrition and the "farm kitchen" were improved with girls being the major agents of change.

According to Wessel and Wessel (1982), youth's openness to new ideas from science had multiple effects. Youth's success with new practices helped farmers overcome their wariness of novel methods while giving youth a well-founded sense of efficacy and leadership. Corn and Tomato Clubs morphed into the 4-H program of the Extension Service of the USDA (Wessel & Wessel, 1982, p. 7). National membership in 4-H caught on quickly and grew to 169,000 by 1916. When America entered the First World War, the need for increased agricultural production pushed up 4-H membership to 500,000.

Empowered by their success in revolutionizing agriculture, youth not only threw themselves enthusiastically into enhanced farm production but became leaders in "public forums to discuss reasons why the United

States was fighting [for democracy] on such distant shores" (Wessel & Wessel, 1982, p. 61). Crosby (1906, p. 574) reached a similar conclusion:

> The influence upon the communities at large, the parents as well as the children, has been wholesome. Beginning with an awakening of interest in one thing--better seed corn-the communities extended their interest to other features of rural improvement, with the result that in the regions affected by the boys' agricultural club movement there has come about a general upward trend to the thoughts and activities of the people.

This observation accords with more contemporary data indicating that youth who participated in 4-H programs in the United States and Canada developed into adults who became active members and leaders of civic organizations (Collins & Associates, 1997; Ladewig & Thomas, 1987). It also fits with youth's openness to what science nowadays says about the role of humans in our changing environment. Whereas many adults are loath to change their views toward human responsibility and nature, more young people are aware of the scientific consensus and open to grapple with consequent policies.

CONCLUSION

We have argued that the environmental issues society faces are serious but cannot be resolved by science alone, by for-profit interest groups, or government agencies. Citizens whose health, employment, and sense of justice (e.g., Hallman, 1994; Quiroz-Martinez, Wu, & Zimmerman, 2005) are involved, must contribute to the debates and the solutions. We believe that raising environmental education to the level of environmental civics can produce citizens who are knowledgeable about issues, have a sense of agency, and care about the issues society faces. There are compelling demonstrations of environmental civics in action, some of which were reviewed earlier.

Contemporary youth are entering a future in which cultural, ethnic, and economic diversity threaten common purpose (see chapter 7). This adds to the importance that schools take up environmental civics that prepares all students for responsible participation in community regulation of community environmental resources. We cited research that suggests that environmental degradation puts at risk the future of communities throughout the world. However, there is compelling research suggesting that community members can be brought together by concern for community resources, to identify with their fellow members, to negotiate about the fair and responsible use of community resources, and to hold each other accountable for abiding by the agreements consensually reached. We believe that community civics can help youth acquire these skills, values, and identities.

Although there is a dearth of systematic, compelling evidence to demonstrate that environmental civics works everywhere effectively, we provided contemporary and historical examples demonstrating that youth can contribute to and learn from participation in science-based efforts to improve the environments in their communities. The openness of youth to new ideas and new strategies allows them to be enthusiastic partners in efforts to protect the environment from new threats and to seize new opportunities for citizenship.

6

Lower the Voting Age and Increase Participation

In May 2013 the city council of Takoma Park, a small city in Maryland, passed legislation lowering the voting age for municipal elections from 18 to 16 (Powers, 2013).[1] It was the first city in the United States to lower the voting age to below 18. The legislation was the subject of much discussion among members of the council, citizens in the city, and students in the high school. Teachers in the school district reported that the lowered voting age made civics discussions meaningful, particularly in relation to the role of citizens in democracy (Generation Citizen, 2016). The community's discussion of the importance of the youth vote combined with the opportunity to cast a ballot mobilized Takoma Park's youth. In the two regular municipal elections subsequent to the lowering of the voting age, 16- and 17-year-olds in Tacoma Park have voted at rates two to three times higher than that for all registered voters (Generation Citizen, 2016). This is particularly remarkable because, as noted in chapter 3, young voters traditionally vote at exceptionally low rates in municipal elections.

1. Portions of this chapter were drawn from Hart, D. & Atkins, R. (2011). American Sixteen- and Seventeen-Year-Olds Are Ready to Vote. *The ANNALS of the American Academy of Political and Social Science, 633*(1), 201–222.

We have argued that adolescents respond to opportunities and that around the world voting is viewed by young people as an important responsibility. Teenagers in England overwhelming believe that voting shapes national governance (Nestle Family Monitor, 2003), and the vast majority of Canadian high school students report that they would vote if they were given the right to do so (Anderson & Goodyear-Grant, 2008). We argue in this chapter that this opportunity—the right to vote—ought to be accorded to those 16 years of age and older. Our argument on behalf of lowering the voting age proceeds in two steps. First, we make the normative argument that 16- and 17-year-olds have the capacities required by classical notions of citizenship. Second, we explore the benefits that will likely arise from lowering the voting age for the community and for the civic development of teenagers.

16- AND 17-YEAR-OLDS ARE CITIZENS

Connotations of citizenship. In the philosophical literature, citizenship is largely defined by three qualities: rights, participation, and membership (Bellamy, 2008). Membership refers to the sense of belonging to the nation and communities of which one is a citizen. Citizens are entitled to rights by virtue of membership, and as citizens they shape these rights through participation in the political process. Full citizenship requires participation in the life of a society.

The criteria for legal citizenship in the United States, and the steps necessary to obtain it for those who do not have it, are intended to ensure that the three elements of citizenship discussed above—membership, concern for rights, and participation—are manifest. Consider the U.S. naturalization law that requires that a candidate be "attached to the principles of the Constitution of the United States, and well disposed to the good order and happiness of the United States" (U.S. Department of Homeland Security, 1952b). The requirement for "attachment" to the principles of the Constitution clearly emphasizes the importance of membership for citizens. To be a citizen is not only to know about the Constitution but also to identify with its underlying principles. Attachment implies a visceral commitment of the individual, the result of which is that the individual is emotionally invested in the principles and, presumably, motivated to enact and defend them.

The processes by which citizenship can be obtained in the United States seem less directly oriented toward participation, perhaps because some forms of civic participation may be required by laws (jury duty, for example), while others are generally viewed as strictly voluntary (service in the military). Nonetheless, the requirement that potential citizens demonstrate a minimal level of civic knowledge seems intended to ensure that the foundation for informed civic action is present.

Political scientists (e.g., Craig, Niemi, & Silver, 1990; Niemi, Craig, & Mattei, 1991) have identified other dispositions that are important for motivating civic and political participation. For example, political skills facilitate participation; knowing how to participate effectively in the political system may be just as important in energizing voting, lobbying, and so on as are possession of the facts about the political system. Political efficacy, reflected in the beliefs that one is an effective political actor, is one of the most widely studied characteristics of voters and citizens and is related to participation. Political and civic interest is also crucially important as those who are interested in community and national news possess more civic knowledge and are more likely to participate in civic life. That an ideal citizen is knowledgeable about the political system, possesses the skills to engage with the system effectively, feels that his or her efforts have impact, and shows an interest in the functioning of the community seems consistent with, if not specified by, philosophical connotations of citizenship.

Moreover, these qualities appear to be psychologically interconnected; they are not simply qualities that legislators and theorists admire. Civic knowledge, political efficacy, and political action are mutually reinforcing. Knowledge contributes to the sense of oneself as an individual who can contribute to the political process, which in turn motivates civic action. Civic action, in turn, contributes to political efficacy and efforts to acquire political knowledge (see Finkel, 1987).

Legal and political notions of citizenship overlap in their emphases on the importance of membership, concern for rights and values, and participation. Although legal constructions of citizenship surely have arbitrary elements, this brief exposition illustrates how facets of requirements for citizenship in the United States reflect broad, widely shared, historically meaningful notions of citizenship. It follows, therefore, that according citizenship has implications for the individual and the political institutions to which he or she belongs. Citizenship is important, and it ought to be accorded to all who are deserving but should not granted to those who are unable to fulfill the responsibilities of citizenship.

Sixteen- and 17-year-olds are indistinguishable from young adults in relevant capacities. In chapters 1, 4, and 5, we reviewed claims that effective civic education demanded imagining youth as citizens rather than as a class of individuals who someday will possess the qualities that allow for participation in society. In this chapter, we extend that line of reasoning by examining the distinction currently made between those 18 years of age and older and those who are younger. This review serves as a foundation for our claim that 16- and 17-year-olds are just as deserving of the vote as those who are slightly older.

One approach to determining the age threshold for voting is to compare age groups on each side of the threshold to determine whether there are differences relevant to citizenship and voting between the two groups. For example, a proposal to move the age threshold for voting from 18 to 21 could be defended by demonstrating that 21-year-olds have better developed qualities necessary for effective voting than do 18-year-olds. We use this approach to compare the qualities associated with citizenship and voting in mid-adolescence to those in late adolescence and early adulthood. In the analyses that follow, we examine the developmental trajectories for *civic knowledge, political interest, political efficacy,* and *participation.* Each of these qualities is a reflection of citizenship as described above.

While civic knowledge is acquired rapidly over the course of childhood and early adolescence, by age 16 the rate of expansion has nearly halted. Bloom, Hill, Black and Lipsey (2008) used nationally standardized tests administered to children and adolescents to estimate how much subject matter growth occurred over the course of each year of elementary and high school for reading, math, science, and social studies. The metric they used is *effect size*, the standardized mean difference in scores between adjacent grades, to index the amount of cognitive growth. The details of the metric do not matter here; the central finding relevant here is clearly evident in Figure 6-1.

Immediately evident in Figure 6-1 is that the rate of cognitive growth on measures of social studies and reading declines precipitously across the school years. As important for our purpose is that the graph signals that there is nearly no improvement on measures of cognitive growth between grades 11 and 12. Said another way, 16- and 17-year-olds—the average age in grade 11—learn very little about social studies (or reading) before turning age 18.

Surprisingly little is learned after age 18 as well. For these comparisons, we draw on data from the 2006 Civic and Political Health Survey (CPHS), which had a nationally representative sample of more than 2,000 young people between the ages of 15 and 25.

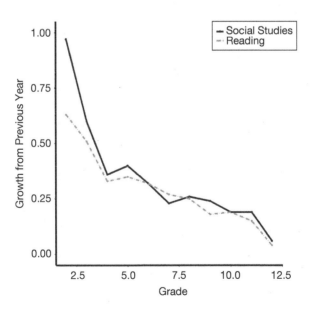

Figure 6-1. Cognitive growth in social studies and reading as a function of school grade.

Political knowledge was assessed in the CPHS with questions such as "would you say that one of the parties is more conservative than the other on the national level? If yes, which is more conservative?" (a correct answer required identification of the Republican Party), "please name one of the president's cabinet secretaries," and "identify the department they represent" (correct responses to each were recorded separately). As is evident in Figure 6-2 below, 16- and 17-year-olds know on average as much about the political system as do 21- and 22-year-olds. There is little in Figure 6-2 to indicate that slightly older, currently enfranchised young adults are better prepared in terms of knowledge about the political system to vote responsibly than are 16- and 17-year-olds (for a similar conclusion based on data from an older study, see Hart & Atkins, 2011).

Political interest in the CPHS was measured with the item:

Some people seem to follow what's going on in government and public affairs most of the time, whether there's an election or not. Others aren't that interested. Do you follow what's going on most of the time (coded as "3"), some of the time ("2"), rarely ("1"), or never ("0")?

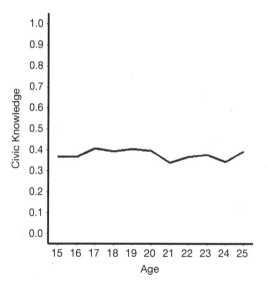

Figure 6-2. Civic knowledge as a function of age.

Figure 6-3 depicts average interest in politics for each year of age. There is little indication of substantial increase in political interest across the course of late adolescence; while it is true that 16-year-olds are least interested in politics, their level of interest is only marginally lower than that of 20- and 22-year-olds. Indeed, it might be argued that if 16-year-olds were given the right to vote, their interest in politics might increase (we review evidence later in the chapter relevant to this possibility). The age trend in Figure 6-3 suggests that political interest peaks at age 18. This is the youngest age at which Americans can now vote. It seems possible that this peak in political interest is a consequence of the newly acquired right to vote, and consequently that if the age for voting was lowered, then the peak in political interest might occur at a younger age.

Political efficacy in the CPHS is revealed by judgments in response to the question:

Thinking about the problems you see in your community, how much difference do you believe YOU can personally make in working to solve problems you see--a great deal of difference (coded as "2"), some difference ("1"), or no difference at all? ("0")".

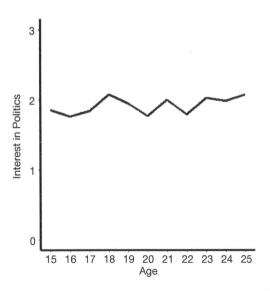

Figure 6-3. Interest in politics as a function of age.

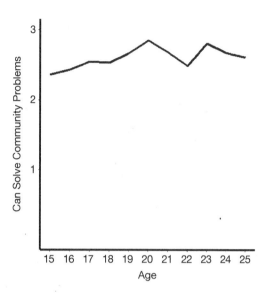

Figure 6-4. Political efficacy as a function of age.

Average scores by age are depicted in Figure 6-4. Political efficacy does seem to increase across the teen years—lowest at age 15, peaking at age 20—but 16- and 17-year-olds experience themselves to be as effective as 22- and 25-year-olds.

Civic participation was measured in two ways in the CPHS. First, youth were asked if they had "contacted or visited a public official—at any level of government—for assistance or to express your opinion?" Those who reported never having done so were coded as "0" while those who had contacted a public official received a "1" for the question. Figure 6-5 presents the percentage of respondents at each year of age who reported having contacted a public official. It appears that 16- and 17-year-olds are just as likely to have expressed their opinions to public officials, or to have sought help from them, as young adults in their early twenties.

Civic participation through volunteering was also assessed in the CPHS. Respondents were asked "have you ever spent time participating in any community service or volunteer activity . . . in the last 12 months?"

On this marker of civic participation, 16- and 17-year-olds are more deserving of the vote than are young adults in their twenties, as is evident in Figure 6-6.

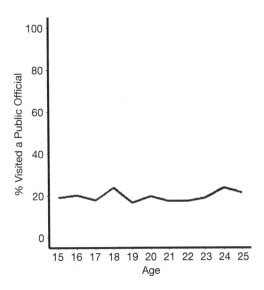

Figure 6-5. Percentage of the population who had visited a public official as a function of age.

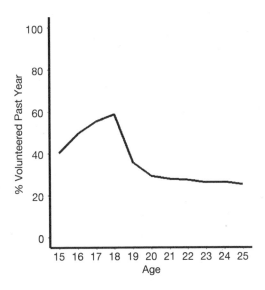

Figure 6-6. Percent who volunteered in the past year, as a function of age.

The evidence from the survey suggests that 16- and 17-year-olds are prepared to vote responsibly. On measures of civic knowledge, political interest, political efficacy, and participation in public civic life, 16-year-olds, on average, are obtaining scores similar to those of adults.

WHAT BENEFITS ACCRUE FROM ENFRANCHISING 16- AND 17-YEAR-OLDS?

Representation of the interests of young people. The changing demographics of American society are central in the argument for extending the vote to 16- and 17-year-olds. Over the last 50 years, the age structure of the United States has changed dramatically (Shrestha & Heister, 2011. For example, the proportion of the population composed of children (those younger than 18) was nearly 50% higher in 1960 (approximately 36% of the population was 17-years-old or younger then) than it is in 2010 (the estimate is that 24% of the American population is under the age of 18) (see Federal Interagency Forum on Child and Family Statistics, 2009). As the percentage of children has declined, the percentage of older adults has increased. These demographic changes in the structure of American society set up the possibility for diverging political interests between young and old.

The American National Election Studies (ANES) have data against which the possibility of diverging political interests between young and old can be judged (American National Elections Studies Time Series Cumulative Data File, 2010). The ANES has data concerning voting and political attitudes dating back to the 1940s. We have used the cumulative data file to examine the association of age to political attitudes concerning federal funding for social security, public schools, and financial aid for colleges. We selected these three topics because of their manifest interest to citizens of different ages. Participants in the ANES were asked whether federal spending in each of these areas ought to be increased (coded "1"), decreased (coded "–1"), or kept about the same (coded "0"). We assume in these analyses that 16- and 17-year-olds would resemble 18- to 24-year-olds in their interests. We graphed the average score for 18- to 24-year-olds

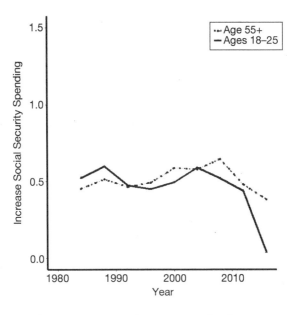

Figure 6-7. Support for increases in social security spending by age group and year.

who voted (because only those who vote have their interests directly represented) for each attitude as well as the average for voters between the ages of 65 and 74—an age bracket that is expanding rapidly.

Figure 6-7 depicts historical trends in support of federal spending in social security by age group. Perhaps contrary to what might be predicted (Bergstrom & Hartman, 2005), for much of the last 30 years, the young and old have been similar in their advocacy for federal support for social security. Surprisingly, then, there is little historical evidence that younger voters differ from older voters in the level of support for social security—a major federal program that benefits, primarily, older Americans.

However, younger and older voters differ substantially in attitudes concerning support for education. Figure 6-8 illustrates average support for federal funding of public schools for the two age groups of voters over the past 30 years. At each measurement point, younger voters view federal funding of public schools more favorably than do older voters.

These differences likely have real implications for public policy. Poterba (1998) reviewed research suggesting that school districts with large fractions

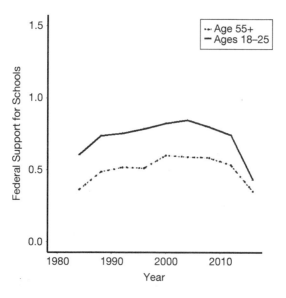

Figure 6-8. Support for federal spending for schools by age group and year.

of older voters are less likely to approve increases in school budgets than are districts with small fractions of older voters—a finding consistent with the trends illustrated in Figure 6-8. Moreover, Poterba described reports indicating that older voters were particularly unlikely to support increases in school budgets when the ethnic makeup of the school-aged population was substantially different than that of the older voters. Brunner and Johnson (2016) also found that age interacts with ethnicity in California voters. Using a sample of 8,000 potential voters in 2008 and 2011, they looked at responses to a question on willingness to pay higher taxes that were needed for state colleges and universities. Younger voters showed more support for higher education than did older voters. Additionally, older non-Hispanic white voters showed greater antipathy to higher taxes when they lived in districts where the college-eligible population was heavily Hispanic. Brunner and Johnson further analyzed actual votes taken on bond referenda for local community colleges. Between 2002 and 2011 there were votes on bonds in 65 or California's 72 community college districts. Results showed that non-Hispanic older white voters varied in their support for bonds in proportion to the percentage of the college age population that was Hispanic in their district. The demographic trends in the United States suggest that the ethnic composition of children and youths will be increasingly diverse (Johnson & Lichter, 2010); if the observations reported by Poterba (1998) are correct—that aging white voters are not inclined to support public schools serving ethnically diverse populations—then enfranchising 16- and 17-year-olds may be particularly important as a means of representing the interests of those enrolled in schools.

Finally, Figure 6-9 illustrates support for increased environmental spending for young and older Americans, drawing again on data from the ANES.

Again, the graph suggests that the rise and fall of support for environmental spending follows the same trajectory for young and old, although younger Americans are generally more supportive of federal funding for this purpose than are older Americans. These data give credence to our proposal in chapter 5 by showing that young people are open to addressing environmental issues.

What these graphs suggest is that if the attitudes of 16- and 17-year-olds are similar to those 18- to 24-year-olds who vote, and the former

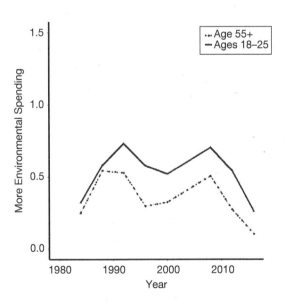

Figure 6-9. Support for federal spending on the environment by age group and year.

were also enfranchised, then there would be more public support among voters for federal spending on public schools and colleges and the environment. Undoubtedly, there are other issues that divide the electorate by age; indeed, in recent years young voters are considerably more liberal than older voters (Taylor & Keeter, 2010). Given that the relative size of the young age group has declined sharply over the past 40 years, and the relative size of the older age groups is increasing substantially, it may be more important now than ever before to extend the vote to 16- and 17-year-olds in the United States. As Johnson and Lichter (2010, p. 169) note, over the past 40 years "the social and economic realities of children [have] deteriorated while the circumstances of the elderly [have] improved." This has happened, we suggest, because the fraction of voters who are elderly has increased, and this group has used its right to vote to advance its interests. One way to improve the circumstances of children and adolescents is to allow their members who are capable of voting responsibly—16- and 17-year-olds—the opportunity to use the electoral process to improve the future prospects of youths.

Can teens vote effectively? It is possible for teenagers to have policy preferences and political interests and yet be without the capacity to select appropriately candidates for electoral office to advance those interests. For example, young people value the role of the federal government in funding public education but might cast their votes for deeply conservative politicians who want to cut federal funding for schools.

It is difficult to assess the extent to which individuals vote wisely. Indeed, Achen and Bartels (2016) demonstrated that voters are swayed by completely random events such as natural disasters and are shockingly ignorant of national issues. Nonetheless, in this chapter the argument is normative rather than descriptive. In fact, there is little evidence that 16- and 17-year-olds are any worse at selecting electoral candidates to advance their interests than are older voters. Wagner, Johann, and Kritzinger (2012) inspected survey data collected from Austrian teenagers and adults in 2008. In 2007 Austrian 16- and 17-year-olds were given the right to vote; consequently, every Austrian 16 years old and older surveyed in 2008 was potentially a voter. Those who reported voting identified the political parties of the candidates that they had voted for. Respondents also rated themselves on a scale running from 0–10 in terms of political orientation (from liberal to conservative). Those who reported voting for candidates of political parties ideologically close to self-rated political orientations were judged to have cast their votes wisely. Wagner and colleagues found that 16- and 17-year-olds were just as likely to vote for candidates of political parties closest to their ideological orientations as were older voters. By this inexact measure of effective voting it appears that 16- and 17-year-old voters are just as able to integrate policy preferences with electoral decisions as are much older voters.

Participation deepens civic commitment. Zeglovits and Zandonella (2013) investigated the effects of enfranchising 16- and 17-year-olds on political interest. In 2007 the Austrian government lowered the general voting age from 18 years old to 16, and mandated at the same time that schools deepen civic education. There was extensive media coverage of the possible effects of the lowered voting age on electoral outcomes as the first election for which the the lowered voting age would be material approached. Zeglovits and Zandella measured political interest with two items administered to a large cohort of 16- and 17-year-olds in 2004 (before the change in voting age) and to another cohort in 2008 (following the change). One item asked, "how interested are you in politics?" with teenagers responding by choosing one of four options: "not at all interested," "not very interested," "fairly interested," or "very interested." The percentage of 16- and 17-year-olds reporting being either "fairly interested" or "very interested" doubled from 2004 (31%) to 2008 (62%). Teenagers also reported the frequency with which they followed the news using a five-point scale ranging from "never" to "every day." In 2004, 37% of 16- and 17-year-olds reported following the news less often than once a week; in 2008, only 19% of teenagers were similarly disengaged. Zeglovits and Zandonella attribute the substantial increase in political interest among 16- and 17-year-olds between 2004 and 2008 to enfranchisement and the associated school-based civic enrichment activities.

Voting begets voting. Plutzer (2002) has argued that voting is best understood from a developmental perspective. Although traditional research on voting focuses on the personal assets which predispose people to vote (education, income, home ownership) and the costs that inhibit voting (distance from the polling station, presence of children at home, work schedules, and so on), Plutzer advocated for viewing voting as a habit acquired over time. Some never acquire the habit; others have the habit interrupted by life circumstances; and in many the habit becomes ingrained, resulting in regular voting. Introducing 16- and 17-year-olds into voting can be the first step to creating habitual voters.

There is now a substantial research base demonstrating that voting is indeed habitual. Atkinson and Fowler (2014) examined the effects of the temporal proximity of election days to religious holidays in Mexico and found that elections held on or within a day of a religious holiday had fewer voters than elections temporally more distant from holidays. More importantly, the effect reverberated through subsequent elections. Recent work has focused on the long-term effects of voting in the teen years on electoral participation in adulthood. Coppock and Green (2015) reviewed many of these studies and conducted their own analyses using a regression-discontinuity design. Teenagers whose birthdays permitted them to vote in national elections shortly after turning 18 years of age were more likely to vote in early adulthood than were slightly younger teenagers who had to wait years to vote in their first national elections. All these findings indicate that voting is to some extent an acquired habit.

There are good reasons to imagine that the habit of voting can be created in mid-adolescence. Holbein and Hillygus (2016) studied the effects of preregistering to vote among 17-year-olds in the United States. Preregistering to vote is allowed in some states; it permits 16- and 17-year-olds, too young to vote legally, to register to vote ahead of their 18th birthdays. Holbein and Hillygus estimate that young adults afforded the opportunity to commit to future voting through preregistration as 16- and 17-year-olds were more likely to vote than were other young adults in states or time periods in which preregistration was not available. Indeed, it is the effectiveness of preregistration in increasing voting rates among young voters, who in recent years tend to vote for Democratic candidates, that may have led Republican legislators in North Carolina to repeal the preregistration law (McClelland, 2016). The habit of voting, it appears, is strengthened even by small steps.

Sixteen- and 17-year-olds vote in other countries. Since 2007 those 16 and older have been allowed to vote in all elections in Austria. The law lowering the voting age to 16 was accompanied by new regulations for improved civic education intended to engage teenagers in the voting process (Zeglovits & Aichholzer, 2014). Zeglovits and Aicholzer used the passage of the age-lowering legislation to examine first-time voting rates in municipal elections among those who are 16- or 17- years of age (who became eligible to vote following legislation in 2007) at the time and 18- or 19-year-olds (prior to 2007). These analyses indicate that the 16- and 17-year-olds were substantially more likely to vote when first age-eligible to do so than were the 18- and 19-year-olds. This finding suggests that younger teenagers can be motivated to vote when allowed to do so. Wagner and Zeglovits (2014) reviewed the effects of extending the vote to 16- and 17-year-olds in Austria and concluded that "that there is little risk and much to gain from giving 16-year-olds the vote." As the experience of other countries with lowered voting ages expands and research accumulates, it will be possible to characterize the consequences of expanded voting ages more precisely.

ARGUMENTS AGAINST EXTENDING THE VOTE TO 16-YEAR-OLDS

A variety of reasons have been offered in opposition to allowing 16- and 17-year-olds to vote.

Lack of Maturity

Not every researcher agrees with our claim that 16- and 17-year-olds ought to vote. For example, Bergh (2013) compared 16- and 17-year-olds to 18-year-olds on measures of political interest and political efficacy and found the younger teenagers to be lacking. Our graphs in this chapter suggest the same pattern. The limitation of Bergh's work, however, is that he assumed that political maturity increases linearly after age 18, with 19- and 20-year-olds even more advanced over 16- and 17-year-olds than the 18-year-olds. But as our graphs earlier in the chapter indicate, this is not always the case; indeed, 16- and 17-year-olds seem to have as much political knowledge as 20-year-olds (Figure 6-2).

McAllister (2014) examined historical data on the effects of lowering the voting age from age 21 to 18 from around the world and reports that 18-year-olds typically vote at lower rates than those who are older. McAllister also compares the political interest and knowledge of young adults (18–24) to that of older adults in Australia and finds that the younger age group fares poorly. This is true as well in the United States; as discussed in chapter 1, young adults vote at lower rates and are less interested in electoral politics than older adults. Perhaps such evidence might buttress an argument for *raising* the voting age (a point McAllister notes). But for the most part these findings are irrelevant for a discussion of extending the voting age downward. As we noted earlier, the evidence from Austria suggests that if allowed to vote, 16-year-olds are more likely to do so than are 18-year-olds. Moreover, in terms of political interest, knowledge, and efficacy, 16- and 17-year-olds are for the most part indistinguishable from 18-year-olds. As far as we know, there is no serious consideration anywhere in the world to raise the voting age so as to exclude currently enfranchised 18- and 19-year-olds from the electorate.

Public Opinion

Chan and Clayton (2006) have suggested that one important issue is whether the general public supports an extension of voting privileges to this new group. There are no survey data on this issue in the United States (to the best of our knowledge), so it is difficult to judge with any precision the degree to which such a proposal would be supported by the American electorate. Extending the vote to 16- and 17-year-olds does not seem to attract much discussion in the media, so it seems safe to conclude that it is not an idea that is of widespread appeal. Certainly there would need to be some public support for enfranchising 16- and 17-year-olds for the idea to be discussed seriously and to mobilize political action.

Yet the extent of prevailing public support for the idea cannot stand by itself as the criterion for deciding whether to enfranchise younger voters. Once a public discussion concerning the idea is underway, public support might shift. Moreover, public opinion on a matter such as extending the vote to 16- and 17-year-olds also reflects self-interests. To the extent that American adults prefer not to enfranchise younger Americans, because such a step might increase public funding toward public schools and college (for example) and consequently raise taxes, public support for allowing 16- and 17-year-olds to vote seems an inappropriate criterion. Denying women the right to vote—people who met the criteria for citizenship and who were capable of voting responsibly—was wrong even when the enfranchised males opposed it.

Neurological Immaturity

Contemporary explanations of teenagers' behavior often refer to the "teenage brain." A great deal of research over the past 25 years has demonstrated that neurological maturation is not complete until early adulthood, an established finding that has played an important role in shaping criminal punishment in the United States. Steinberg (2013) examined Supreme Court decisions banning capital punishment and life imprisonment for those younger than 18 years of age, and found that evidence of neurological immaturity in teenagers was quite important to the court. The immaturity of adolescents' brains has been offered as an important reason for teenagers' involvement with drugs, risky driving, unprotected sex, and aggression (Casey, Jones, & Hare, 2008). Findings linking adolescent neurological immaturities to the behaviors of teenagers seem to emerge daily.

One surprising consequence of this research is that adolescents are increasingly viewed through the frame of brain development. There are podcasts, magazine articles, television shows, news stories, books with the theme that neurology is the key to understanding teenagers (for example, Jensen and Nutt's (2015) *The Teenage Brain: A Neuroscientist's Survival Guide to Raising Adolescents and Young Adults* is among the top-selling books in the adolescence category at Amazon as we write this chapter). As Bessant (2008) pointed out, viewing teenagers as beings controlled by immature brains culminating in inappropriate, risky action leads to a number of undesirable conclusions, among them that the voting age should be raised to the age of full maturation (mid to late twenties), rather than lowered.

There are at least several reasons why the temptation to understand adolescents as neurologically impaired humans ought to be resisted. The first of these is that brains of teenagers resemble those of adults more than they differ. Adolescent brain function is perhaps distinctive in its sensitivity to reward and arousal (Casey, Jones, & Hare, 2008), with this sensitivity manifest in diminished cognitive control when emotions are extreme (Cohen, et al., 2016). Although it is likely true that adolescents' capacities to restrain impulsive, emotional behavior may be reduced relative to that of adults, these capacities do not figure prominently in citizenship and particularly in voting. Neither the sense of membership, the concern with rights, nor the ability to participate in the community rest heavily upon the ability to resist emotional, impulsive actions. Citizenship and voting in the electoral process require, for the most part, decisions made over long periods of time, which allows for deliberation and discussion with others. To date, there is no neurological evidence that indicates that 16- and 17-year-olds lack the requisite neurological maturation necessary for citizenship or for responsible voting; nor is there evidence to indicate that a breadth-of-life experience is necessary for effective citizenship.

Developmental differences between the brains of adolescents and adults probably should not all be characterized as resulting in adolescent deficits. There are a variety of cognitive tasks that adolescents are much better at than middle-aged and elderly adults. Hartshorne and Germine (2015) administered a wide variety of measures used to assess facets of intelligence and found that on many of them, teenagers scored higher than most adults; on many more tasks they found that that teenagers performed better than did elderly adults. While performance on these tasks is unclearly linked to brain maturation, our point is that if adolescents are generally better at these tasks than adults, it seems unlikely that the brains of adolescents can be characterized as vastly immature relative to those of adults.

CONCLUSION

Sixteen- and 17-year-olds in the United States ought to be permitted to vote in local and national elections. This claim rests upon the exploration of the notion of citizenship, in some of its legal meanings in the United States as well as its connotations in political philosophy. Citizens should be entitled to vote, unless there is good reason to believe that they cannot fulfill their responsibilities as citizens or as voters. The research reviewed in this chapter, as well as the new analyses that were presented, demonstrate that 16- and 17-year-olds are generally indistinguishable in their capacities to function as citizens and to vote responsibly from the youngest adults (18-year-olds) who are entitled to vote. The implication is that to deny 16- and 17-year-olds the right to vote is arbitrary.

Extending the right to vote to 16- and 17-year-olds is particularly important at this point in American history. The proportion of the American population composed of children has declined dramatically in the last 40 years, while the fraction of older voters, who are less inclined to support policies beneficial to the interests of children and youth, is increasing rapidly. By enfranchising 16- and 17-year-olds, the political power of children and adolescents would be increased and perhaps necessarily so to balance the growing population of older voters.

Finally, the right to vote is an *opportunity* to which 16- and 17-year-olds will respond. Enfranchising 16- and 17-year-olds will enhance motivation to learn about civics (see the decline in learning from grade 10 to 12; Figure 6-1) make high school civics education much more meaningful. It is known that simulations such as mock courts and discussion of issues enhance civic learning (Guilfoile & Delander, 2014). How much more, then, can having responsibility as voters bring relevance to civic education! Moreover, youth who can vote will be solicited by those who want to be elected, opening opportunities for young people to engage in meaningful dialogue with those who lead their communities. Finally, the right to vote will likely deepen adolescents' interest in acquiring civic knowledge while it strengthens their civic habits. By removing an arbitrary barrier to their full participation in society, enfranchising 16- and 17-year-olds adds to the moral legitimacy of our democracy.

We do not know why a century ago political scientists and educators were so ready to treat high school students as regular citizens with rights and responsibilities rather than as voters in the distant future (see Committee Reports of the American Political Science Association from 1908, 1916, 1922). But we believe it is worth reviving their perspective by granting the vote to 16- and 17-year-olds. It would acknowledge their citizen status, bring them directly into the civic sphere, and start them on a path of sharing governance responsibility with adults. The results are likely to be an awakening of youth's interest in politics at the moment when they are defining their identities in relationship to society. They would begin to think of themselves as citizens with a real stake in politics (Levine, 2012). Isn't that what our democracy sorely needs?

7

Civic Development in
the 21st Century

C ivic and political life in the United States is fraying. Trust in government is at near historic lows (Pew Research Center, 2015), the
presidential race of 2016 revealed deep divisions among segments
of the American population, and the U.S. Congress is so riven by schism
that it barely functions. In chapter 2, we explored some of the reasons for
these disturbing trends and concluded that systemic problems inhibit the
political system from quick rebound to full citizen participation and effective functioning on behalf of citizens. No doubt the trends and the genesis
of the problems are sources of the lack of interest in politics among youth
and young adults.

Our premise is that we must promote civic development among our
youth. Young people deserve this opportunity, and our communities need
the strength that well-prepared citizens will bring. As noted in chapters 1
and 3, young people vote at low rates, distrust government, and are
increasingly disengaged from community life. And as argued in chapter 4,

traditional civic education has not altered this bleak picture. If young people withdraw from civic life, their interests will increasingly be ignored by political leaders (chapter 6). Moreover, our political system, strangled into ineffectiveness by growing ideological polarization, is desperately in need of fresh leadership of the type that could be provided by young adults—if they were positioned to enter into public life in greater numbers.

It might be argued that our premise is wrong. Perhaps youth participation in civic life will increase without intervention, obviating the need for solutions we proposed in chapters 5 and 6; maybe the ideological polarization crippling the federal government will recede without the infusion of new citizens with different values into the system. But the trends concerning youth participation and political polarization on which our premise rests are systemic and long term (chapter 2). As we noted earlier, diminishing youth interest in civic participation and increasing ideological polarization have been occurring for decades. Speculating that the future will be better is not a solution.

We foresee the path to full participation in civic life becoming more challenging. Entry into civic participation is easiest in settings where members share interests and meet regularly to collaborate on common goals. The farther a community is from this ideal, the more difficult it is for adolescents to feel joined to civic life. As we noted earlier, deep ideological divisions already wrack the federal government and inhibit a sense of common purpose. More problematic, however, are two challenges to contemporary life: demographic-economic transitions and transformations in community institutions.

DEMOGRAPHIC AND ECONOMIC TRANSITIONS

The United States is a different country than it was fifty years ago. There are schisms resulting from economic inequality and different kinds of community segregation. When members of communities are pulled apart from one another, the sense of common community purpose often recedes. Both income inequality and segregation stretch the community's fabric. As income inequality increases, the interests of groups with a lot of money diverge from others that are poorer. Similarly, segregation within communities—groups within a community differing on one dimension or another separated socially from each other—breeds between-group competition.

Income inequality. Economic inequality has been rising in the United States for the last fifty years. Whether income inequality is character-ized by the percentage of wealth possessed by the richest one-tenth of one percent in the country (e.g., Saez & Zucman, 2014) or by income (e.g., Stone, Trisi, Sherman, & Horton, 2016), the picture is clear: the difference between the haves and the have nots has steadily increased since the 1970s. Although it is certainly possible for those who are enor-mously rich and those who are poor to share common interests, there will be instances in which what is best for those who are affluent will diverge from the interests of their less fortunate neighbors. We already noted in chapter 2 that rich people are far more successful in influencing elected officials than poor people are. But income inequality is perni-cious for civic participation in other ways. Across a number of countries, high income inequality is associated with exaggerated gaps in academic achievement and educational attainment, both of which are associated with civic participation. It is certainly difficult to identify each link in the causal chain from income inequality to performance in school. But it is surely safe to infer that children and teenagers desperately poor by the standards of their community can feel hopeless and alienated—neither of which is optimal for learning.

Further, income inequality is regularly associated with diminished civic participation (Lancee & Van de Werfhorst, 2012) and measures of community well-being (Wilkinson & Pickett, 2010). Lancee and Van de Werfhorst looked at the relation between economic inequality across states within the European Union and participation in civil society groups. They reported that the greater the inequality, the lower the rate of participation. Wilkison and Pickett (2010) found that inequality, whether measured within nations or within states in the United States was associated with lower levels of social trust and physical and mental health.

Racial and ethnic segregation. Demographic forecasts for the United States suggest that present-day minority groups are increasingly large fractions of the population, foretelling that cultural change is almost sure to follow. Since the 1970s (see Figure 1-1), immigration has increased sharply, resulting in more cultural and religious diversity. This mix poses a serious challenge to achieving mutual understanding and makes "civic republicanism" in quest of the common good a serious challenge (Flanagan, 2013; Tienda, 2002). Unless specific mechanisms are put in place to bring about mutual understanding and trust, the pro-social act of working together for a common purpose can fragment into defensive stances of self-preservation.

Through much of the 20th century, the "common public school" functioned to some degree, as it was intended in the 19th century, as an asset for democracy (Bryk, Lee, & Holland, 1993). With obvious exceptions, youth from different racial, immigrant, religious, and economic statuses attended classes together, experienced a common curriculum, and developed a shared culture and character. But today, even as racial and ethnic diversity has expanded, the ideal of the common school has dimmed. As the Government Accounting Office (GAO, 2016) noted, "The percentage of K-12 public schools in the United States with students who are poor and are mostly Black or Hispanic is growing." The inevitable consequence of this form of segregation is the demise of the common public school as a place where young people of different backgrounds congregate together for learning.

Allen (2004) argued that the basis of democracy lies in recognizing the connections between costs and rewards in the contributions of many people. Acknowledgement of this fact may be difficult to achieve because of "differences of position, experience, and perspective" (p. xix). Racial and economic division are two factors that impede appreciation of our interdependence as citizens. This becomes more evident under the ethos that celebrates individual solo achievement in a context where people in respective groups have little personal contact and remain separated from generation to generation (see Sharkey, 2013, regarding Chicago). Allen uses the metaphor of *political friendship* to illustrate where this process should lead. Friends practice reciprocity while acknowledging their respective differences, say, in temperament or background. Nevertheless, they accept them for the sake of maintaining their relationship as an end in itself. Political friendship extends this concept to "strangers" or the host of other citizens who belong the whole of our democracy.

Allen's (2004) perspective sets a high bar because it pictures democracy as more than accepting legal bounds on rivalrous interests. Allen wants citizens' "allegiance to wholeness" (p. 88) and a "willingness to sacrifice some of one's power for the sake of common agreement" (p. 93). The key to seeing and accepting this quest for wholeness is grasping how our acts are reciprocally related in what is basically a "consensually based political community" (p. 97). All of these qualities are harder to realize when minorities are segregated in poor schools, and many wealthy young people are educated in select enclaves.

Even decidedly less rational, less deliberative, theories about the functioning of American democracy underscore the dangers of economic and racial segregation. Achen and Bartels (2016) dismissed the possibility that American democracy does or can operate through reflective, informed, deliberation among citizens and argue instead that citizen participation is largely influenced by social identities. Each person can have many social identities. Some reinforce others, but these identities may also be in conflict. Throughout we have suggested that a central goal for civic development is the formation in young people of a citizen identity, an image of oneself with bonds with and responsibilities to other people. The citizen identity motivates civic participation and makes public life in a society possible. Segregation submerges the citizen identity beneath the social identities made salient by separation: the haves, the have nots, whites, Hispanics, natives, immigrants, and so on. Whether one imagines that democratic rule will best function as citizens join in reflective, deliberative friendship with each other—or by assuming social identities that incorporate responsibilities to others—segregation can only be corrosive.

A CHANGING ORGANIZATIONAL STRUCTURE

Political socialization requires building skills and knowledge that allow the individual to enter into mature political life. As discussed in earlier chapters, and demonstrated in numerous studies (e.g., Hart, Donnelly,

Youniss, & Atkins, 2007), adolescents connected to neighborhood institutions are more likely to acquire civic skills and participate in their communities. These organizations provide rationales for action, offer training for competent engagement in civic life, and facilitate action when it is needed.

At the start of the 21st century, two important studies documented the historical fate of organized groups in the United States. In the well-known 2000 study, *Bowling Alone*, Robert Putnam (2000) offered extensive evidence showing that formal, fraternal, and even informal groups such as bowling leagues had reached a peak near the mid-20th century and then declined rapidly thereafter. These groups had provided the lifeblood of everyday civic life by bringing people from various sectors of society together where they interacted, got to know one another, and formed bonds of trust. Most of these groups were not formally political in purpose, but they served the democratic enterprise by confirming broad common interest and turning potential strangers into fellow and sister citizens.

In an equally important study, Skocpol (2003) plotted the trajectory of membership groups (e.g., Parent Teacher Associations; the American Legion; Elks; the Women's Christian Temperance Union) that were organized into federations spanning the country. Their growth, which began in the mid-19th century, reached a high point in the mid-20th century and then tailed off. These fraternal, charitable, and interest groups specified credentials for membership and ran according to rules of order that were shared across local chapters. Members participated collectively in making decisions and learned the basics of democracy such as how to speak publicly, carry on civil debate, vote for plans of action, and abide peaceable changes in leadership through elections. The federated structure connected one group to another in a branching from local to state, then regional to federal levels. In this regard, these groups mirrored the interconnected structure of local to national government. The data for these groups show a pattern similar to that reported by Putnam with a significant decline occurring after the 1960s and 1970s.

Skocpol proposed that these groups gave way to a new kind of "membership" that was based on interest but occurred at a distance without direct participation in decision making. Arising before the Internet, these groups took the general form of having small professional staffs that were supported by financial contributions from members scattered across the country but sharing interest, say, in the environment (e.g., Sierra Club), aging and health issues (e.g., American Association of Retired People), or child well-being (e.g., Children's Defense Fund). The staffs, often housed near relevant government agencies, formed policy, did lobbying, helped shape public opinion, and devised programs for public education on pertinent issues. Members were contacted by mail and by publications; in return members sent in money. This new kind of structure is exemplified by AARP, which at the start of the 21st century claimed 33 million members, had a legislative staff of 169 professionals, maintained 28 lobbyists, and had 1,200 workers in the field (Skocpol, 2003).

As membership organizations dependent on interacting individuals gave way to "direct-mail" organizations run by experts, civic engagement in the broad sense, including voting, began to ebb. This trend occurred even though educational attainment increased, and higher levels of education are usually associated with increased civic participation (Rosenstone & Hansen, 1993). With government appearing more distant and with policy being formed by expert-professionals, it is no wonder that individual efficacy has waned (American National Election Studies, 2010). It would be odd if this citizen passivity did not spread to youth who, as we saw, are not central objects of interest to the major parties and take on focus only periodically when voters are mobilized (Shea, 2009; Shea & Green, 2007). If policy favors those with wealth and power (Gilens, 2011) and is viewed as the province of experts, youth are all the more entitled to feel left out. But as we argued, there are ways to bring youth back into politics with meaningful roles.

Despite the loss of civic organizations overall, there is healthy civic organizational life precisely in the environmental domain. It would provide youth with roles that contribute to policy as full-fledged citizens. For example, Johnson, Agnone, and McCarthy (2010) found that passage of major environmental legislation, the Clean Air and Clean Water Acts, were in part products of policy produced by professional organizations in tandem with protests and demonstrations of citizens at the local community level. This fact supports our belief that encouraging youth participation and granting them the right to vote locally would facilitate their civic development. Their involvement would bring them fully into decisions that affect their communities of residence, from schools to health to public safety to transportation.

Our view is in keeping with recent concerns expressed about the relationship between the changing meaning of "membership" and the power of distant expertise. Slaughter and Scott (2015) observed that the rise of "think tanks" as centers for policymaking may have overstepped reasonable bounds. It has recently been reported that model legislation is framed by central ideological machines then sent out to the states, bypassing local circumstances and citizens, in the process (Hertel-Fernandez, 2016). Although technical expertise is surely needed for many contemporary issues (an insight voiced in 1922 by Walter Lippmann), its cost is too high when it occludes the experiences of average citizens. Some scholars acknowledge this by calling for a new kind of relationship in which professional experts realign with the vitality and expertise of local civic organizations that deal in the nitty-gritty of need, opportunity, and civic spirit (Slaughter & Scott, 2015). We agree, and that is why we believe an active form of citizenship can be cultivated if youth were made part of existing civic life.

IS THE INTERNET THE ANSWER?

We are now well into the Internet age in which self-directed, unedited communication has given power to individuals. As new technologies developed, hypotheses flowed regarding their potential to engage young people who increasingly showed disinterest in traditional sources of political information, such as network television and daily newspapers, (Wattenberg, 2012). Early on, it was recognized that these technologies could be used to mobilize large numbers of people in more efficient and effective ways than mass advertising or direct mail solicitation could when it came to entertainment, public safety, or the spread of ideas (Shirky, 2008). Given the low voter turnout documented in chapter 3, scholars raised the question as to whether these technologies could become the solution for reengaging young people, since they had adapted to them so readily (Milner, 2010; Hindmann, 2009). This possibility took on fresh relevance during the 2004 presidential primary campaign when Howard Dean's campaign team employed the Internet successfully for fundraising and voter registration (Friess, 2012). Four and then eight years later, these tactics were refined and became even more effective in the successful campaigns of Barack Obama. His youth supporters raised money, registered, and turned out in large numbers, easily outpacing the youth turnout associated with his opponent (Starks, 2017).

In retrospect, these early successes may be seen as promises of a better future through empowerment of individuals that would circumvent old authority centers and multiply into an engaged generation of youth. Subsequent research suggests that emphasis on individual capacity was too narrow a focus to serve the end of involvement because it based success on imagined coordinated political action arising spontaneously without the mediation of structured organization (Karpf, 2012; Neuman, Bimber, & Hindman, 2011). Some scholars envisioned a renaissance led by youth who would start petitions, create content, raise issues, and connect people in like-thinking groups. And all of this would be accomplished with relatively minimal staff or money compared with federated groups, direct mail campaigns, and think tanks. Eventually, these groups would give way to self-defined individual-generated groups that cohered on particular issues or candidates.

The excitement of the possibilities of the Internet for deepening civic engagement and empowering social movements (e.g. Kahne, Ullman, & Middaugh, 2012; Tolbert & McNeal, 2003) have yielded to the realities that there is no single effect of the electronic world on civic participation, and in any event most of these effects are relatively minor (for a review, see Boulianne, 2009). It is unlikely that Internet-based communication of any form will resolve the problems besetting American politics and youth civic engagement in the foreseeable future. For example, in a clever experimental study of the effects of social media on voting, Bond et al. (2012) studied voting-relevant information presented via Facebook. Some users of Facebook received no treatment; this was the control group. Other Facebook users received information about voting (for example, where they could vote—this was the information intervention group), while other users were informed about how many other Facebook users had already voted and information about their Facebook friends who had reported voting (social intervention group). Those in the social intervention group were fractions of a percentage point more likely to vote than those in first group (the sample size of 6 million for this analysis allowed reliable detection of even small effects like this). In some respects, the findings of this study are remarkable: that even brief messages on Facebook can influence voting is fascinating and important. On the other hand, there is little in this set of findings to suggest that civic engagement will be readily transformed by digital communications. The Internet possesses a variety of tools—it is easily accessible, used daily by young people, and capable of connecting people with shared interest—that may contribute to civic engagement in the future. Perhaps in a decade or so there will be enough research to identify how the Internet can be leveraged to reinvigorate civic development. But we are unaware of compelling research to indicate that the promotion of civic development ought to be shifted to digital platforms in the early 21st century.

ENGAGING YOUTH

We have argued throughout that provided with the right opportunities, youth will participate in civic life. There is nothing intrinsic to adolescence—no deficits of neurological maturation nor life experience—that inhibit youth from political and civic life. We need these opportunities more than ever, if our identification of challenges to entry into civic life detailed in the previous section are at all accurate.

It is worth remembering that youth have been key civic and political actors throughout American history. In the 1850s, for example, older children and adolescents were active, vocal participants in American politics. Grinspan (2016) documented that "from 1840 to 1900, young people fueled American politics." The leadership and energy young people contributed to American politics in the late 19th century were not a reflection of mysteriously acquired generational characteristics but a direct consequence of the opportunities provided by politics and political parties. Grinspan (2016) wrote that

> some young people cared about shaping policy, others turned out for 'fun and frolic,' but nearly all used their political system to achieve personal goals. In a tumultuous era, underage activists and first-time voters saw that public politics could help their private lives. They could find friends, mentors, identity and entertainment, advancement and even romance at rallies. Young Americans fueled their political system, not out of youthful idealism, but because all of their individual hopes accumulated to make them a public force.

While Grinspan's account may give less credence to civic motivation than others might, his broad claim that the openness of the political system and political parties to the contributions of youth and the rewards for participation were crucially important, resonates with our own. Youth need not be dragged into civic life; under the right circumstances, they will flock to it and energize it.

Youth were key civic actors in the 20th century as well. For example, youth powered the civil rights movement, providing many of its leaders, workers, and in some respects its inexhaustible moral courage (e.g., Halberstam, 1998). With passing time this era of American history is more read about than personally recalled, so it is easy to overlook the contributions of youth to one of the most important social movements ever to occur in the United States (Fendrich, 1993; McAdam, 1988). But in fact, young people gave life to a movement that offered them meaningful opportunities to contribute to social change, and in doing so contributed to political reform and cultural transformation throughout the country.

This same era provides two other examples of youth activism driven by ideals and a quest for justice. Progressive politics was exemplified by the Students for Democratic Action whose political manifesto (Port Huron Statement, 1962), addressed explicitly how young people, facing a faltering society, would renew its democratic spirit. One goal of political change was to "bring people into community in order that they find meaning" (Port Huron Statement, 1962). In 1960 youth on the political right took an equally strong stand on how to save the America they envisioned. In the preamble to their affirmation of American political principles (the Sharon Statement, 1960), conservative young people asserted that it was "the responsibility of the youth of America to affirm eternal truths" that included "God-given free will," the "right to be free," and the connection between political freedom and economic free markets (see also Andrew, 1997).

It would be wise not to dismiss this moment of history as an exaggerated case of youthful hubris. In fact, these three groups of young people effected lasting changes on the American landscape. Moreover, the participants in these three movements maintained lifelong commitments to political activism and change (see Andrew, 1997, on the Young Americans for Freedom; Braungart & Braungart, 1991, on the Young Americans for Freedom and the Students for a Democratic Society; Fendrich 1993 and McAdam, 1988, on civil rights participants; and Jennings, 2002, on youth engaged peace and anti-nuclear movements).

From our perspective as scholars of youth development, these examples clearly show the meeting of the psychology of identity with political theory (Malin, Ballard, & Damon, 2015; Yates & Youniss, 1999). As youth are confronting their personal skills, frailties, and ideals, they look to how they fit into society and think about the kind of society in which they would want to live. At this developmental moment, moral and political ideals are brought to bear on self-reflection in a potent way. According to Malin and her colleagues., this is the moment when youth confront how society interconnects us and in our context of democracy, our interdependence brings to salience concepts of liberty, justice, and equality. It is known that during adolescence, these concepts are well within the cognitive reach of youth (Flanagan, 2013). The question is how to activate them in such a way as to help youth see themselves as citizens within a democratic framework. For us this requires putting youth into the civic-political fray where they can "fight out among and within themselves contending ideas of the meaningful life and ... discover that self-interest need not be at odds with concern for one another" (Delbanco, 2012, p. 177).

ENVIRONMENTAL CIVICS AND VOTING

We have offered environmental civics and the right to vote as opportunities that can energize youth to participate in American civic life. Neither singly nor together will these lift youths' involvement to the levels seen in the 1850s or the 1960s. But we are convinced that these are the right steps to take and can be a foundation to build on. We will not review the details of our arguments here—we provided them in chapters 5 and 6—but it is worth remembering that youth are genuinely interested in environmental issues and in voting. There is vibrant youth participation in any number of environmental organizations, and youth are deeply involved in organizing efforts to lower the voting age to 16 in communities throughout the United States (in the fall of 2016, campaigns were underway in San Francisco and Berkeley, for example).

Moreover, the environment and the vote are key. Chapter 5 briefly discussed environmental degradation as crucially important for all societies. Already global warming is imperiling millions of people living near oceans or who depend upon seasonal rainfalls for subsistence farming. Young people are more inclined to think about these issues than are older Americans; we need their best thinking on the environment, combined with their skills and commitments, if widespread catastrophes are to be avoided.

Without the right to vote, young people are at increased risk for being ignored in the political process. Already political parties devote few resources to recruiting young people; as the country grows older, and more ethnically diverse, young people will become invisible in the political process. By allowing younger people to vote, the number of teenagers eligible to vote will double. Politicians will become more interested in the youth block, creating more opportunities for youth participation and youth influence. Moreover, allowing 16- and 17-year-olds to vote is the right thing to do. As we demonstrated in chapter 6, there are no meaningful differences in political competence between 16- and 17-year-olds, currently not permitted to vote, and 18-year-olds who can. Lowering the voting age will increase the legitimacy of our political system.

We do not believe that hope alone will improve youth civic participation or American politics. As we discussed in chapter 4, schools, currently assigned primary responsibility for preparing American citizens, are far less successful than most understand. Schools can do better, of course, and improvement in them could be one product of high-quality research. But we think civics education would be dramatically improved with experiences of responsible environmental action and by lowering the voting age, which would then make civics education in high school relevant. Talking about a vote one will cast in a month's time enlivens discussion of current events in a way that a potential vote to occur several years in the future years will not.

The solutions we have proposed do not reform youth, nor stamp civic virtue into them. Neither is necessary. Young people today have the aptitudes and skills necessary to contribute to their communities; what they need are the appropriately structured opportunities that adults, schools, civil society organizations, and government can provide.

Youth can be an enormous asset to civic life. They have served this function previously in American history. They can do so in our future. Now is a critical moment to make it possible for young people to once again renew American democracy.

REFERENCES

Abramowitz, A. I. (2013). The electoral roots of America's dysfunctional government. *Presidential Studies Quarterly, 43*(4), 709–731.

Abramowitz, A. I. (2010). *The disappearing center: Engaged citizens, polarization, and American democracy.* New Haven, CT: Yale University Press.

Abramowitz, A. I., & Saunders, K. L. (2008). Is polarization a myth? *Journal of Politics, 70*(2), 542–555.

Achen, C. H., & Bartels, L. M. (2016). *Democracy for realists: Why elections do not produce responsive government.* Princeton, NJ: Princeton University Press.

American Civil Liberties Union, (2003). ACLU wins settlement for New Mexico teachers punished for posting anti-war materials. Retrieved from https://www.aclu.org/news/aclu-wins-settlement-new-mexico-teachers-punished-posting-anti-war-materials

Aftermath: Sixteen *New Yorker* writers on Trump's America. (n.d.). Retrieved from http://www.newyorker.com/magazine/2016/11/21/aftermath-sixteen-writers-on-trumps-america

Allen, D. (2004). *Talking to strangers: Anxieties of citizenship since Brown v. Board of Education.* Chicago: University of Chicago Press. Retrieved from https://books.google.com/books?hl=en&lr=&id=eZiGS807wAEC&oi=fnd&pg=PP10&dq=allen+political+friendship&ots=y5u4ruolh-&sig=se4FuaN5lDS0v3XA4uNB58oloE0

Alperovitz, G., & Speth, J. G. (2011). *America beyond capitalism: Reclaiming our wealth, our liberty, and our democracy.* Takoma Park, MD: Democracy Collaborative Press.

American National Election Studies. (2010). *American National Election Studies. TIME SERIES CUMULATIVE DATA FILE.* Stanford University and the University of Michigan. Retrieved from http://www.electionstudies.org/studypages/cdf/cdf_funding.htm

Anderson, C. D., & Goodyear-Grant, E. (2008). Youth turnout: Adolescents' attitudes in Ontario. *Canadian Journal of Political Science, 41*(3), 697–718.

Andrew, J. A. (1997). *The other side of the sixties: Young Americans for Freedom and the rise of conservative politics.* New Brunswick, NJ: Rutgers University Press.

Atkinson, M. D., & Fowler, A. (2014). Social capital and voter turnout: Evidence from Saint's Day fiestas in Mexico. *British Journal of Political Science, 44*(1), 41–59. https://doi.org/10.1017/S0007123412000713

Bamberg, S., & Moser, G. (2007). Twenty years after Hines, Hungerford, and Tomera: a new meta-analysis of psycho-social determinants of pro-environmental behaviour. *Journal of Environmental Psychology*, *27*(1), 14–25.

Barber, C., Sweetwood, S. O., & King, M. (2015). Creating classroom-level measures of citizenship education climate. *Learning Environments Research*, *18*(2), 197–216.

Bartels, L. M. (2009). *Unequal democracy: The political economy of the new gilded age.* Princeton, NJ: Princeton University Press.

Baumgartner, F. R., Berry, J. M., Hojnacki, M., Kimball, D. C., & Leech, B. (2009). *Lobbying and policy change: Who wins, who loses and why.* Chicago: University of Chicago Press.

Bellamy, R. (2008). *Citizenship: A very short introduction.* Oxford: Oxford University Press.

Bergh, J. (2013). Does voting rights affect the political maturity of 16-and 17-year-olds? Findings from the 2011 Norwegian voting-age trial. *Electoral Studies*, *32*(1), 90–100.

Bergstrom, T. C., & Hartman, J. (2005). Demographics and the political sustainability of pay-as-go Social Security. CESinfo Working paper series No. 1378. https://papers.ssrn.so13/papers.cfm?abstract_id=648523

Bershidsky, L. (2016, October 23). Democracy turns off millennials. It doesn't have to. *Bloomberg View.* Retrieved from https://www.bloomberg.com/view/articles/2016-10-23/democracy-turns-off-Millennials-it-doesn-t-have-to

Bessant, J. (2008). Hard wired for risk: Neurological science, "the adolescent brain" and developmental theory. *Journal of Youth Studies*, *11*(3), 347–360.

Bloom. H. S., Hill, C. J., Black, A. B., & Lipsey, M. W. (2008). Performance trajectories and performance gaps as achievement effect size benchmarks for educational interventions. *Journal of Research on Educational Effectiveness*, *1*(4), 289–328.

Bond, R. M., Fariss, C. J., Jones, J. J., Kramer, A. D. I., Marlow, C., & Settle, J. E., et al. (2012). A 61-million-person experiment in social influence and political mobilization. *Nature*, *489*(7415), 295–298. https://doi.org/10.1038/nature11421

Boulianne, S. (2009). Does Internet use affect engagement? A meta-analysis of research. *Political Communication*, *26*(2), 193–211. https://doi.org/10.1080/10584600902854363

Boyte, H. C. (2004). *Everyday politics: Reconnecting citizens and public life.* Philadelphia: University of Pennsylvania Press.

Braungart, M. M., & Braungart, R. G. (1991). The effects of the 1960s political generation of former left- and right-wing youth activist leaders. *Social Problems*, *38*(3), 297–315.

Brennan, J. (2016). *Against democracy.* Princeton, NJ: Princeton University Press.

Bryk, A. S., Lee, V. E., & Holland, P. E. (1993). *Catholic schools and the common good.* Cambridge, MA: Harvard University Press.

Brunner, E. J., & Johnson, E. B. (2016). Intergenerational conflict and the political economy of higher education funding. *Journal of Urban Economics*, *91*(1), 73–87.

Bureau of Labor Statistics. (2015). Volunteering in 2014. *TED: The economics daily.* February 27, 2015.

Campaign for the Civic Mission of schools n.d. Retrieved from http://www.civicmissionofschools.org

Campbell, C., & Horowitz, J. (2016). Does college influence sociopolitical attitudes? *Sociology of Education, 89*(1), 40–58. https://doi.org/10.1177/0038040715617224

Campbell, D. E. (2006). What is education's impact on civic and social engagement. In *Measuring the effects of education on health and civic engagement: Proceedings of the Copenhagen symposium* (pp. 25–126). Retrieved from http://www.oecd.org/education/innovation-education/37425694.pdf

Campbell, D. E., Levinson, M., & Hess, F. M. (2012). *Making civics count: Citizenship education for a new generation.* Cambridge, MA: Harvard Education Press.

Campbell, D. E., & Niemi, R. G. (2016). Testing civics: State-level civic education requirements and political knowledge. *American Political Science Review, 110*(3), 495.

Cannan, J. (2013). A legislative history of the ACA: How legislative procedure shapes legislative history. *Law Library Journal, 105*(2), 132–173.

Carney, E. N. (2015). Party unity: Standing together against any action. Retrieved from http://library.cqpress.com/cqweekly/file.php?path=/files/wr20150316-2014_Party_Unity.pdf

Casey, B. J., Jones, R. M., & Hare, T. A. (2008). The adolescent brain. *Annals of the New York Academy of Sciences, 1124*(1), 111–126.

Caughey, D., Dunham, J., & Warshaw, C. (2016). *The ideological nationalization of mass partisanship: Policy preferences and partisan identification in state publics, 1946–2014* (SSRN Scholarly Paper No. ID 2853674). Rochester, NY: Social Science Research Network. Retrieved from https://papers.ssrn.com/abstract=2853674

Chan, T. W., & Clayton, M. (2006). Should the voting age be lowered to sixteen? Normative and empirical considerations. *Political Studies, 54*(3), 533–558.

Chappell, E. (2017). Posters deemed anti-Trump removed from Westminster High classrooms. Retrieved from http://www.carrollcountytimes.com/news/education/ph-cc-westminster-hs-politics-20170217-story.html

Chetty, R., Friedman, J. N., & Rockoff, J. E. (2011). *The long-term impacts of teachers: Teacher value-added and student outcomes in adulthood.* National Bureau of Economic Research. Retrieved from http://www.nber.org/papers/w17699

Chilton, D. (2014). Why millennials don't vote. *The Week.* October 31, 2014. The week.com/articles/4427007/why-Millennials-don't-vote

Cinner, J., Huchery, C., MacNeil, A., Graham, N. A. J., McClanahan, T. R., Maina, J., et al. (2016, July). Bright spots among the world's coral reefs. *Nature, 535,* 416–449.

CIRCLE youth volunteering rate much higher than in the 1970s and '80s. (n.d.). Retrieved from http://www.civicyouth.org/youth-volunteering-rate-much-higher-than-in-the-1970s-and-80s/

Citizens United v. Federal Election Commission, No. 08-205 (2010). Cornell University Law School, Legal Information Institute.

Civic and Political Health Survey. (2006). Retrieved from http://civicyouth.org/PopUps/2006_CPHS_Report_update.pdf

Cohen, A. O., Breiner, K., Steinberg, L., Bonnie, R. J., Scott, E. S., & Taylor-Thompson, K. A., et al. (2016). When is an adolescent an adult? Assessing cognitive control in emotional and nonemotional contexts. *Psychological Science, 27*(4), 549–562. https://doi.org/10.1177/0956797615627625

Colby, A., Ehrlich, T.homas; Beaumont, Elizabeth; & Stephens, Jason (2003). *Educating citizens: Preparing America's undergraduates for lives of moral and civic responsibility.* San Francisco: Jossey-Bass.

Colby, A., Beaumont, E., Ehrlich, T., & Corngold, J. (2007). *Educating for democracy: Preparing undergraduates for responsible political engagement.* San Francisco: Jossey-Bass.

Collins, J. B., & Associates. (1997). *Measures of success: a project of the Canadian 4-H Council measuring impacts of 4-H programs on members, families and alumni.* Ottawa, Canada: Canadian 4-H Council.

Coppock, A., & Green, D. P. (2015). Is voting habit forming? New evidence from experiments and regression discontinuities. *American Journal of Political Science.* https://doi.org/10.1111/ajps.12210

Council of Economic Advisors. (n.d.). 15 ECONOMIC FACTS ABOUT millenials. Retrieved from https://www.whitehouse.gov/sites/default/files/docs/Millennials_report.pdf

CQ. (2014). CQ Roll Call's vote studies—2013 in review. Retrieved from http://www.media.cq.com/votestudies.

Craig, S. C., Niemi, R. G., & Silver, G. E. (1990). Political efficacy and trust: A report of the NES pilot study items. *Political Behavior, 12*(3), 289–314.

Crain, C. (n.d.). The case against democracy. Retrieved from http://www.newyorker.com/magazine/2016/11/07/the-case-against-democracy

Crick Report. (1998). *Education for citizenship and the teaching of democracy in schools.* Final report of the Advisory Group on Citizenship. Retrieved from http://www.dera.ioe.ac.uk/4385/1/crickreport/1998.pdf.

Crittenden, J., & Levine, P. (2013). Civic education. In Edward N. Zalta (Ed.), *The Stanford encyclopedia of philosophy.* Retrieved from http://plato.stanford.edu/archives/sum2013/entries/civic-education/

Crosby, D. J. (1906). *Boys agricultural clubs. Washington: U. S. Department of Agriculture,* Office of Experiment Stations. Retrieved from https://archive.org/stream/boysagricultural00cros/boysagricultural00cros_djvu.txt

Current Population Survey. (2015). Volunteering Supplement. Retrieved from http://www.icpsr.umich.edu/icpsrweb/NADAC/studies/36411

Cutler, D. M., & Lleras-Muney, A. (2006). *Education and health: evaluating theories and evidence.* National Bureau of Economic Research. Retrieved from http://www.nber.org/papers/w12352

Dalton, R. J. (2008). Citizenship norms and the expansion of political participation. *Political Studies, 56*(1), 76–98. https://doi.org/10.1111/j.1467-9248.2007.00718.x

Dalton, R. J. (2009). *The good citizen: How a younger generation is reshaping American politics.* Washington, DC: CQ.

Davenport, D. (n.d.). No, we shouldn't lower the voting age to 16. Retrieved from http://www.forbes.com/sites/daviddavenport/2016/05/25/no-we-shouldnt-lower-the-voting-age-to-16/

Dawes, C. T., Settle, J. E., Lowen, P. J., McGue. M, & Iacano (2016). Genes, psychological traits and civic engagement. *Philosophical Transactions B.* Retrieved from http://rstb.royalsocietypublishing/org

Delbanco, A. (2012). *College, what it was, is, and should be.* Princeton, NJ: Princeton University Press.

Dewey, S. (n.d.). Wage premium from college is said to be up. Retrieved from http://economix.blogs.nytimes.com/2014/02/11/wage-premium-from-college-is-said-to-be-up/

Dewey, J. (1916). *Democracy and education: an introduction to the philosophy of Education.* New York: Macmillan.

Diener, E., Sandvik, E., Seidlitz, L., & Diener, M. (1993). The relationship between income and subjective well-being: relative or absolute? *Social Indicators Research, 28*(3), 195–223.

Dietz, T., Ostrom, E., & Stern, P. (2003). The struggle to govern the commons. *Science, 302*(5652), 1907–1912.

Drutman, L. (2005). How corporate lobbyists conquered American democracy. *The Atlantic.* Retrieved from http://www.theatlantic.com/business/archive/2015/04/how-corporate-lobbyists-conquered-American-democracy/390822/

Duffett, A. M., Miller, C., Hess, F. M., Schmitt, G. J., Talbot, J. S., & Farkas. S. (2010). *High schools, civics, and citizenship: what social studies teachers think and do.* Retrieved from https://www.aei.org/publication/high-schools-civics-and-citizenship/

Dunn, A. R. (1910). *Civics, the community and the citizen.* Retrieved from https://archive.org/details/civicscommunity00dunngoog.

Eastman, W. D. (1999). *The influence of immigration on the development of civic education In the United States from 1880-1925.* MA Thesis, Harvard University, Cambridge, MA.

Edelstein, W. (2011). Education for democracy: Reasons and strategies. *European Journal of Education, 46*(1), 127–137.

Edwards, M. (2012). *The parties versus the people.* New Haven, CT: Yale University Press.

Egelko, B. (2007). 'Honk for peace' case tests limits on free speech. Retrieved from http://www.sfgate.com/news/article/Honk-for-peace-case-tests-limits-on-free-speech-2594488.php

Einstein, K. L., & Kogan, V. (2016). Pushing the city limits: Policy responsiveness in municipal government. *Urban Affairs Review, 52*(1), 3–32.

Elchardus, M., & Spruyt, B. (2009). The culture of academic disciplines and the sociopolitical Attitudes of students: a test of selection and socialization effects. *Social Science Quarterly, 90*(2), 446–460.

Englehardt, E. (2009, Winter). Canning tomatoes, growing 'better and more perfect women': The girls Tomato Club movement. *Southern Cultures,* 78–92.

Environmental Protection Agency, Environmental Education. Retrieved from https://www.epa.gov/education/what-environmental-education

Fang, L. (2014, February 19). Where have all the lobbyists gone? *The Nation.* Retrieved from http://www.thenation.com/article/shadow-lobbying-complex

Feldman, L., Pasek, J., Romer, D., & Jamieson, K. H. (2007). Identifying best practices in civic education: Lessons from the student voices program. *American Journal of Education, 114*(1), 75–100.

Fendrich, J. M. (1993). *Ideal citizens: The legacy of the civil rights movement.* Albany: State University of New York Press.

Ferreira, F., & Gyourko, J. (2009). Do political parties matter? Evidence from US cities. *Quarterly Journal of Economics, 124*(1), 399–422.

Generation Citizen. (2016). Final-MD-Case-study.pdf. (n.d.). Retrieved from http://vote16usa.org/wp-content/uploads/2016/10/Final-MD-Case-Study.pdf

Finkel, S. E. (1987). The effects of participation on political efficacy and political support: Evidence from a West German panel. *Journal of Politics, 49*(2), 441–464.

Finn, C. E., Jr. (2003). Foreword. In Leming, J., Ellington, L., & Porter-Magee, K.(Eds.), *Where did social studies go wrong.* Thomas B. Fordham Foundation. Retrieved from http://www.edexcellence.net/doc.ContrariansFull.pdf

Fiorina, M.s P., Abrams, S. J., & Pope, J. C. (2006). *Culture war? The myth of polarized America.* New York: Pearson Longman

Fitchett, P. G., & Heafner, T. L. (2010). A national perspective on the effects of high-stake Testing and standardization on elementary social studies marginalization. *Theory & Research, 38*(1), 114–130.

Flake, J., & Heinrich, M. (2014, October 21). Two opposing senators, a deserted island and an idea. *Washington Post.* Retrieved from https://www.washingtonpost.com/opinions/two-opposing-senators-a-deserted-island-and-an-idea/2014/10/21/127ef9e6-579c-11e4-bd61-346aee66ba29_story.html

Flanagan, C. A. (2013). *Teenage citizens: The political theories of the young.* Cambridge, MA: Harvard University Press.

Foa, R. S., & Mounk, Y. (2016). The democratic disconnect. *Journal of Democracy, 27*(3), 5–17.

Friedland, L. A., & Morimoto, S. (2005). *The changing lifeworld of young people: risk, resume-padding, and civic engagement.* Working paper 40. Center for Information, Research, and Civic Engagement. College Park: University of Maryland.

Frostenson, S. (2017, January 22). The women's marches may have been the largest demonstration in US history. Retrieved from http://www.vox.com/2017/1/22/14350808/womens-marches-largest-demonstration-us-history-map

Gallay, E., Marckini-Polk, L., Schroeder, B., & Flanagan, C. (2016). Place-based stewardship Education: nurturing aspirations to protect local commons. *Peabody Journal of Education, 92*(2), 155–175.

Gallup (2003, March 24). Retrieved from http://www.gallup.com/poll/8038/seventytwo-percent-americans-support war-against-iraq.aspx

Galston, W. (2001). Political knowledge, political engagement, and civic education. *Annual Review of Political Science, 9*(4), 217–234.

Garofoli, J. (n.d.). YOUTH VOTE/Young voters preferred Kerry, but turnout wasn't high. Retrieved from http://www.sfgate.com/politics/joegarofoli/article/YOUTH-VOTE-Young-voters-preferred-Kerry-but-2676968.php

Gates Foundation. (n. d.). Measures of effective teaching. Retrieved from http://k12education.gatesfoundation.org/teacher-supports/teacher-development/measuring-effective-teaching/?gclid=CL2Z39PRx9ICFUhYDQodsvgJ3Q

Geboers, E., Geijsel, F., Admiraal, W., & ten Dam, G. (2013). Review of the effects of citizenship education. *Educational Research Review, 9*, 158–173.

Gelber, A., Isen, A., & Kessler, J. B. (2014). *The effects of youth employment: Evidence from New York City Summer Youth Employment Program lotteries.* National Bureau of Economic Research. Retrieved from http://www.nber.org/papers/w20810

Generation Citizen. (2016). LOWERING THE VOTING AGE FOR LOCAL ELECTIONS IN TAKOMA PARK AND HYATTSVILLE. Retrieved from http://vote16usa.org/wp-content/uploads/2016/10/Final-MD-Case-Study.pdf

Gilens, M. (2011). *Affluence and influence: Economic inequality and political power in America*. New York: Russell Sage Foundation and Princeton University Press.

Gilens, M., & Page, B. I. (2014). Testing theories of American politics: elites, interest groups, and average citizens. *Perspectives on Politics, 12*(3), 564–581.

Gimpel, J. G., Lay, J. C., & Schucknecht, J. E. (2003). *Cultivating democracy: Civic experiences and political socialization in America*. Washington, DC: Brookings Institution.

Goodman, J. C. (2016, December 20). Why Republicans don't have an Obamacare replacement. *Forbes*. Retrieved from http://www.forbes.com/2016/12/20/why-the-republicans-dont-have-an-obamacare-replacament-plan/#5

Goodman, J., Hurwitz, M., & Smith, J. (2015). *College access, initial college choice and degree completion*. National Bureau of Economic Research. Retrieved from http://www.nber.org/papers/w20996

Greenberg, E. H., & Weber, K. (2008). *Generation we: How millennial youth are taking over America and changing our world forever*. Pachatusan.

Grinspan, J. (2016). *The virgin vote: How young Americans made democracy social, politics personal, and voting popular in the nineteenth century*. Chapel Hill: University of North Carolina Press.

Guilfoile, L. & Delander, B. (2014). Six preventive practices for effective civic learning. Retrieved from http://www.ecs.org/clearinghouse/01/10/48/11048.pdf.

Hacker, J. S., & Pierson, P. (2010). *Winner-take-all politics: How Washington made the rich richer–and turned its back on the middle class*. New York: Simon and Schuster.

Hacker, J. S., & Pierson, P. (2010a). Winner-take-all politics: public policy, political organization, and the precipitous rise of top incomes in the United States, *Politics & Society, 38*(2), 152–204.

Haines, C. G. (1916). *The teaching of government: Report to the American Political Science Association by the committee on instruction*. Retrieved by https://ia801403.us.archive.org/zipview.php?zip=/31/items/olcovers566/olcovers566-L.zip&file=5665540-L.jpg

Halberstam, D. (1998). *The children*. New York: Random House.

Hallman, D. G. (Ed.) (1994). *Ecotheology: Voices from south and north*. Eugene, OR: Wipf & Stock.

Hardin, G. (1968). The tragedy of the commons. *Science, 162*(3859), 1243–1248.

Hart, D., & Atkins. R. (2011). American sixteen- and seventeen- year-olds are ready to vote? *Annals of the American Academy of Political and Social Science, 633*, 201–222.

Hart, D., & Sulik, M. (2014). The social construction of volunteering. In L. Padilla-Walker & G. Carlo (Eds.), *The complexities of raising prosocial children* (pp. 393–413). New York: Oxford University Press.

Hart, D., Donnelly, T. M., Youniss, J., & Atkins, R. (2007). High school community service as a predictor of adult voting and volunteering. *American Educational Research Journal, 44*(1), 197–219.

Hartman, M. (2014, March 24). Millennials at work: Young and callow, like their Parents. *New York Times*. Retrieved from http://www.nytimes.com/2014/03/25/your-money/Millennials-at-work-young-and-callow-like-their-parents.html

Hartshorne, J. K., & Germine, L. T. (2015). When does cognitive functioning peak? The asynchronous rise and fall of different cognitive abilities across the life span. *Psychological Science*. https://doi.org/10.1177/0956797614567339

Hasen, R. L. (2014, April 2) Die another day: The supreme court takes a big step closer to gutting the last bit of campaign finance reform. *Slate*. Retrieved from http://www.slate.com/artile/news-andpolitics/jurisprudence/2014/04/the-subtle-awfulness-of-the-metucheon-v-fee-campaign-finance-decision-the.html

Heller, S. B. (2014). Summer jobs reduce violence among disadvantaged youth. *Science, 346*(6214), 1219–1223.

Helms, S. E. (2013). Involuntary volunteering: The impact of mandated service in public schools. *Economics of Education Review, 36*, 295–310. Retrieved from https://doi.org/10.1016/j.econedurev.2013.06.003

Henderson, A., Brown, S. D., Pancer, S. M., & Ellis-Hale, K. (2007). Mandated community service in high school and subsequent civic engagement: The case of the "double cohort" in Ontario, Canada. *Journal of Youth and Adolescence, 36*(7), 849–860.

Hertel-Fernandez, A. (2016, Winter). How the right trounced liberals in the states. *Democracy, 39.* Retrieved from http://democracyjournal.org/magazine/39/how-the-right-trounced-liberals-in-the-states/

Hess, D. E. (2009). *Controversy in the classroom: The democratic power of discussion.* New York: Routledge.

Hess, D.E., & McAvoy, P. (2015). *The political classroom: Evidence and ethics in democratic education.* New York: Routledge.

Hill, H. C., & Chin, M. (2014).Year-to-Year Stability in Measures of Teachers and Teaching. Center for Education Policy Research. Retrieved from https://cepr.harvard.edu/publications/year-year-stability-measures-teachers-and-teaching

Hindman, M. S. (2009). *The myth of digital democracy.* Princeton, NJ: Princeton University Press.

Hines, J. M., Hungerford, H. R., & Tomera, A. N. (1987). Analysis and synthesis of research on responsible environmental behaviour: A meta-analysis. *Journal of Environmental Education, 18*(1), 1–8.

Holbein, J. B., & Hillygus, D. S. (2016). Making young voters: The impact of preregistration on youth turnout. *American Journal of Political Science, 60*(2), 364–382. https://doi.org/10.1111/ajps.12177

Hooghe, M., Oser, J., & Marien, S. (2016). A comparative analysis of 'good citizenship': A latent class analysis of adolescents' citizenship in 38 countries. *International Political Science Review, 37*, (1), 115–129.

Hooghe, M., & Quintelier, E. (2011). School and country-effects on the political participation intentions of adolescents. A multilevel study of open classroom climate and participatory school culture in 34 countries. Retrieved from https://lirias.kuleuven.be/handle/123456789/314672

Hubert. H. Humphrey Civic Education Enhancement Act (2001-2002). Retrieved from https://www.congress.gov/bill/107th-congress/senate-bill/1238/text

Ingraham, C. (2016). The dramatic shift among college professors that's hurting students' education. Retreived from https://www.washingtonpost.com/news/wonk/wp/2016/01/11/the-dramatic-shift-among-college-professors-thats-hurting-students-education/?utm_term=.4f5dc56839f0

Jacobson, G. C. (2012). The electoral origins of polarized politics: Evidence from the 2010 Cooperative Congressional Election study. *American Behavioral Scientist, 56*(12), 1612–1630.

Jacobson, G. C. (2013). Partisan polarization in American politics: A background paper. *Presidential Studies Quarterly, 43*(4), 688–708.

Jacobson, G. C. (2015). How do campaigns matter? *Annual Review of Political Science, 18*, 31–47.

Jaeger, W. P., Lyons, J., & Wolak, J. (2016). Political knowledge and policy representation in the states. *American Politics Research.* https://doi.org/10.1177/1532673X16657806

Jamieson, K. H. (2013). The challenges facing civic education in the 21st century. *Daedalus, 142*(2), 65–83.

Jennings, M. K. (2002). Generational units and the student protest movement in the United States: An intra- and intergenerational analysis. *Political Psychology, 23*(2), 302–324.

Jensen, F. E., & A. E. Nutt (2015). *The teenage brain: Neuroscientist's guide to raising adolescents and young adults.* New York: HarperCollins.

Johanek, M. C. (2012). Preparing pluribus for unum: Historical perspectives on civic education. In D. E. Campbell, M. Levinson, & F. E. Hess (Eds.), *Making civics count: Citizenship Education for a new generation* (pp. 77–82). Cambridge, MA: Harvard Education Press.

Johnson, E. W., Agnone, J., & McCarthy, J. D. (2010). The contingent impact of U. S. environmental movement organizations and activities on agenda setting and law passage. *Social Forces, 88*(5), 2267–2292.

Johnson, K. M., & Lichter, D. T. (2010). Growing diversity among America's children and youth: Spatial and temporal dimensions. *Population and Development Review, 36*(1), 151–176.

Johnston, A. (2014, October 29). Political peril: Why millennials don't vote. Retrieved from http://www.voxmagazine.com/2014/10/political-peril-why-Millennials-dont-vote/

Kahne, J., Ullman, J., & Middaugh, E. (2012). Digital opportunities for civic education. In D. Campbell, M. Levinson, & F. Hess (Eds.), *Making Civics Count: Citizenship Education for a New Generation* (pp. 207–228).

Karpf, D. (2012). *The MoveOn effect: The unexpected transformation of American political advocacy.* New York: Oxford University Press.

Katz, B., & Bradley, J. (2013). *The metropolitan revolution: How cities and metros are fixing our broken politics and fragile economy.* Washington, DC: Brookings Institution. Retrieved from https://www.brookings.edu/book/the-metropolitan-revolution-2/

Keating, A., & Janmaat, J. G. (2016). Education through citizenship at school: Do school activities have a lasting impact on youth political engagement? *Parliamentary Affairs, 69*(2), 409–429. https://doi.org/10.1093/pa/gsv017

Klemmensen, R., Hatemi, P. K., Hobolt, S. B., Skytthe, A., & Nørgaard, A. S. (2012). Heritability in political interest and efficacy across cultures: Denmark and the United States. *Twin Research and Human Genetics, 15*(1), 15–20.

Kirshner, B. (2015). *Youth activism in an era of education inequality.* New York: New York University Press.

Kirshner, B. & Ginwright, S. (2012). Youth organizing as a context for African American and Latino adolescents. *Child Development Perspectives, 6*(3), 288–294.

Konstnatopoulos, S., & Hedges, L. V. (2008). How large an effect can we expect from school reforms? *Teachers College Record, 110*(8), 1613–1640.

Kudryastev, A., & Krasny, M. E. (2012). *Urban environmental education: preliminary literature review.* Document CEL-2012-1. Ithaca, NY: Cornell University Civic Ecology Lab.

Ladewig, H., & Thomas, J. K. (1987). *Does 4-H make a difference? The 4-H alumni study.* College Station: Texas A & M University.

Lancee, B., & Van de Werfhorst, H. G. (2012). Income inequality and participation: A comparison of 24 European countries. *Social Science Research, 41*(5), 1166–1178. https://doi.org/10.1016/j.ssresearch.2012.04.005

Langton, K. P., & Jennings, M. K. (1968). Political socialization and the high school civics curriculum in the United States. *American Political Science Review, 62*(3), 852–867.

LaPira, T. M., & Thomas, H. F., III (2014). Revolving lobbyists and interest representation. *Interest Groups & Advocacy, 3*(1), 4–29.

Lawless, J. L., Fox, R. L., & Fox, R. L. (2015). *Running from office: Why young Americans are turned off to politics.* New York: Oxford University Pres.

Lenroot, K. (1934). Cited in Paul N. Hanna, *Youth serves the community* (1936). New York: Appleton-Century, p. 267.

Levine, Peter. (2009). "The Civic Opportunity Gap." *Educational Leadership, 66,* 20–25.

Levine, J. F., Hargett, G., McCann, J. P., Potts, D., & Pierre, S. (2011). The Wilson Bay initiative, riverworks, and Sturgeon City partnerships: A case study for building effective academic-community partnerships. *Journal of Higher Education Outreach and Engagement, 15*(3), 121–133.

Levine, P. (2007). *The future of democracy: Developing the next generation of American citizen.* Medford, MA: Tufts University Press.

Levine, P. (2013). *We are the ones we have been waiting for: The promise of civic renewal in America.* New York: Oxford University Press.

Levine, P. (2012). Education for a civil society. In D. E. Campbell, M. Levinson, & F. M. Hess (Eds.), *Making civics count: citizenship education for a new generation* (pp. 37–56). Cambridge, MA: Harvard Education Press.

Levine, P., & Gibson, C. (2003). *The civic mission of schools.* New York: Carnegie Corporation of New York.

Levine, P., Fung, A., & Gastil, J. (2005). Future directions for public deliberation. *Journal of Public Deliberation, 1*(1). Retrieved from http://search.proquest.com/openview/8cd756f4e2db9ad27e4bdf432b014de1/1?pq-origsite=gscholar

Levine, P., & Lopez, M. H. (2002). Youth voter turnout has declined by any measure. *Fact Sheet,* September, 2002. Center for Information and Research on Civic Learning and Engagement.

Levinson, M. (2014). *No citizen left behind.* Cambridge, MA: Harvard University Press.

Levy, B. L. M., Solomon, B. G., & Collet-Gildard, L. (2016). Fostering political interest among youth during the 2012 Presidential Election. *Educational Researcher, 45*(9), 483–495. https://doi.org/10.3102/0013189X16683402

Liebelson, D. (2017, February 21). School asks teachers to take down pro-diversity posters, saying they're 'anti-Trump.' *Huffington Post.* Retrieved from http://www.huffingtonpost.com/entry/school-pro-diversity-posters-trump_us_58ac87b9e4b0e784faa21446

Lippmann, W. (1922). *Public opinion.* New York: Macmillan.

Lopez, M. H., Levine, P., Both, D., Kiesa, A., Kirby, E., Marcelo, K., & Williams, D. (2006). The 2006 civic and political health of the nation. *The Center for Information and Research on Civic Learning and Engagement*. Retrieved from https://pdfs.semanticscholar.org/1185/1fc76c3dbb8c9717eefc4a6bcd6e0f160972.pdf

Maciag, M. (n.d.). Millennials let their grandparents decide local elections. Retrieved from http://www.governing.com/topics/elections/gov-voter-turnout-generations-Millennials.html

Malin, H., Ballard, P. J., & Damon, W. (2015). Civic purpose: An integrated construct for understanding civic development in adolescence. *Human Development, 58*(2), 103–130.

Mann, T. E., & Ornstein, N. J. (2006). *The broken branch: How Congress is failing America and how to get it back on track*. New York: Oxford University Press.

Mann, T. E., & Ornstein, N. J. (2012). *Its even worse than it looks: how the American constitutional system collided with the new politics of extremism*. New York: Basic Books.

Manning, N., & Edwards, K. (2014). Does civic education for young people increase political participation? A systematic review. *Educational Review, 66*(1), 22–45.

Marcelo, K. B., Lopez, M. H., Kenndey, C., & Barr, K. (2008). Young voter registration and turnout trends. Center for Information and Research on Civic Learning and Engagement. Medford: MA.

Martens, A. M., & Gainous, J. (2013). Civic education and democratic capacity: How do teachers teach and what works? *Social Science Quarterly, 94*(4), 956–976.

Maurin, E., & McNally, S. (2008). Vive la révolution! Long-term educational returns of 1968 to the angry students. *Journal of Labor Economics, 26*(1), 1–33.

Mayer v. Monroe County. (2007). 474 F.3d 477 (7th Cir.2007).

McAdam, D. (1988). *Freedom summer*. New York: Oxford University Press.

McAllister, I. (2014). The politics of lowering the voting age in Australia: Evaluating the evidence. *Australian Journal of Political Science, 49*(1), 68–83. https://doi.org/10.1080/10361146.2013.868402

McCrae, R. R., Costa, P. T. Jr., Ostendorf, F., Angleitner, A., Hřebíčková, M., & Avia, M. D., et al. (2000). Nature over nurture: Temperament, personality, and life span development. *Journal of Personality and Social Psychology, 78*, 173.

McKinley, J. C. Jr. (2010, March 12). Texas conservatives win curriculum change. *New York Times* http://www.nytimes.com/2010/03/13/education/13texas.html?mcubz=3.

McIntosh, H., Hart, D., & Youniss, J. (2007). The influence of family political discussion on youth civic development: Which parent qualities matter? *PS: Political Science & Politics, 40*(3), 495–499.

McClelland, M. (2016) Inside the Knock-Down, Drag-out Fight to Turn North Carolina Blue. Mother Jones. Retrieved from: http://www.motherjones.com/politics/2016/09/North-Carolina-voting-rights-hb2-naacp-lgbt-trans-pope.

Mettler, S. (2002). Bringing the state back in to civic engagement: Policy feedback effects of the GI Bill for World War II veterans. *American Political Science Review, 96*(2), 351–365.

Mettler, S., & Welch, E. (2004). Civic generation: policy feedback effects of the GI Bill on political involvement over the life course. *British Journal of Political Science, 34*(3), 497–518.

Metz, E.C., & Youniss, J. (2003). September 11 and service: A longitudinal study of high school students' views and responses. *Applied Developmental Science, 7*(3) 148–155.

Metz, E. C., & Youniss, J. (2005). Longitudinal gains in civic development through school-based required service. *Political Psychology, 26*(3), 413–437.

Milner, H. (2010). *The internet generation: engaged citizens or political dropouts.* Medford, MA: Tufts University Press.

Mitchell, A., Gottfried, J., & Matsa, K. E. (2015). Political interest and awareness lower among millennials. Retrieved from http://www.journalism.org/2015/06/01/political-interest-and-awareness-lower-among-Millennials/

NAEP. (2014). U.S. History, geography, and civics assessments. Retrieved from http://www.nationsreportcard.gov/hgc_2014/#civics/scores

Nestle Family Monitor. (2003). Young people's attitudes toward politics. Retrieved from https://www.ipsos-mori.com/Assets/Dos/Archives/Polls/nfm16.pdf

Neuman, W. R., Bimber, B., & Hindman, M. (2011). The Internet and four dimensions of citizenship. In R. Y. Shapiro & L. Jacobs (Eds.), *The Oxford handbook of American public opinion and the media* (pp. 22–43). Oxford: Oxford University Press.

Niemi, R. G., & Junn, J. (1998). *Civic education: What makes students learn.* New Haven, CT: Yale University Press.

Niemi, R. G., Craig, S. C., & Mattei, F. (1991). Measuring internal political efficacy in the 1988 National Election Study. *American Political Science Review, 85*(4), 1407–1413.

Nonprofit Vote. "America Goes to the Polls: 2016," 2017. Retrieved from : http://www.nonprofitvote.org/documents/2017/03/america-goes-polls-2016.pdf.

Oliver, T. O., Lee, P. R., & Lipton, H. L. (2004). A political history of Medicare and Prescription drug coverage. *Milbank Quarterly, 82*(2), 283–354.

Olsen-Phillips, P., Choma, R., Bryner, S., & Weber, D. (2015). The political one percent of the one percent in 2014: mega donors fuel rising costs of elections. Retrieved from http://www.opensecrets.org/news/2015/04/the-political-one-percent-of-the-one-percent-in-2014-mega-donors

Opensecrets. (2015). 'All cooled off': As Congress convenes former colleagues will be call-- ing from K Street. Retrieved from www.opensecrets.org/news/2015/01/coming-out-of-the-cool-as-congress-convenes-former-colelagues-will-soon-be-calling-from-K-street

Ostrom, E. (2009). Beyond markets and states: polycentric governance of complex economic systems. Retrived from http://www.nobelprize.org/nobel-prizes/laureate/2009/Ostrom-lecture.pdf.

Ostrom, E. (2014). Collective action and the evolution of social norms. *Journal of Natural Resources Policy Research, 6*(4), 235–252.

Ostrom, E. (2015). *Governing the commons.* Cambridge, MA: Cambridge University Press.

Page, B. I., Bartels, L, M., & Seawright, J. (2013). Democracy and policy preferences of wealthy Americans. *Perspective on Politics, 11*(1), 51–73.

Pancer, S. M. (2015). *The psychology of citizenship and civic engagement.* New York: Oxford University Press.

Pancer, S. M., Pratt, M., Hunsberger, B., & Alisat, S. (2007). Community and political involvement: What distinguishes the activists from the uninvolved. *Journal of Community Psychology, 35*(6), 741–759.

PBS. (2010). Texas school board approves controversial textbook changes. Retrieved from http://www.pbs.org/wnet/need-to-know/culture/texas-school-board-approves-controversial-textbook-changes/954/

Pearson, K. (2005). *Party discipline in the contemporary Congress: Rewarding loyalty in theory and practice*. Berkeley: University of California Press.

Persson, M. (2015). Classroom climate and political learning: Findings from a Swedish panel study and comparative data. *Political Psychology*, *36*(5), 587–601.

Pew Research Center,(2017), On Eve of Inauguration, Americans Expect Nation's Deep Political Divisions to Persis. Retrieved from http://assets.pewresearch.org/wp-content/uploads/sites/5/2017/01/19114635/01-19-17-2017-Political-outlook-release.pdf.

Pew Research Center (2012). Youth engagement falls; registration also declines. Retrieved from http://www.pewresearch.org/fact-tank/2013/09/28/youth-engagement-falls-registration-also-declines/

Pew Research Center. (2015). U. S. politics and policy. Retrieved from http:// www.people-press.org/2015/111/23/1-trust-in-government-1958- 2015/

Piketty, T. (2013). *Capitalism in the twenty-first century*. Cambridge, MA: Harvard University Press.

Piketty, T., & Saez, E. (2003). Income inequality in the United States, 1913–1998. *Quarterly Journal of Economics*, *118*(1), 1–39.

Pittman, K. J., Irby, M., Tolman, J., Yohalem, N., & Ferber, T. (2003). *Preventing problems, Promoting development, encouraging engagement*. Washington, DC: Forum for Youth Investment.

Phillips, A. 2016. Is Split-Ticket Voting Officially Dead?. *Washington Post*. Accessed December 12, 2016. https://www.washingtonpost.com/news/the-fix/wp/2016/11/17/is-split-ticket-voting-officially-dead/.

Planty, M., & Regneir, M. (2004). *Volunteer service by young people from high school through early adulthood*. Washington, DC: National Center for Education Statistics.

Plutzer, E. (2002). Becoming a habitual voter: Inertia, resources, and growth in young adulthood. *American Political Science Review*, *96*(1), 41–56.

Poole, K., & Rosenthal, H. (2015). *The polarization of the congressional parties*. https://legacy.voteview.com/Political_Polarization_2014.htm.

Pope Francis. (2015) *Laudato Si: on care for our common home*. Vatican City: Vatican Press.

Pope Francis (2015). *Laudato Si': on care of our common home*. W2.vatica,.va/content/Francesco/em/encyclicals/documents/papa-francesco-20150524_enciclica-lauadto-si.html.

Porter, E. (2013, November 12). Rethinking the rise of inequality. *New York Times*. Retrieved from http://www.nytimes.com/2013/11/13/business/rethinking-the-income-gap-and-a-college-education.html

Porter, E. (2014, September 10). A simple equation: More education = more income. *New York Times*. Retrieved from http://www.nytimes.com/2014/09/11/business/economy/a-simple-equation-more-education-more-income.html

Porterba, J. (1998). Demographic change, intergenerational linkages, and public education. *American Economic Review*, *88*(2), 315–320.

Port Huron Statement of the Students for Democratic Society. (1962). Retrieved from http://coursesa.matrix.msu.edu/~hst306/documents/huron.html

Power, F. C., Higgins, A., & Kohlberg, L. (1991). *Lawrence Kohlberg's approach to moral education*. New York: Columbia University Press.

Powers, L. (2013). Takoma Park grants 16-year-olds right to vote. *Washington Post*. Retrieved from https://www.washingtonpost.com/local/takoma-park-grants-16-year-olds-right-to-vote/2013/05/14/b27c52c4-bccd-11e2-89c9-3be8095fe767_story.html

Prior, M. (2010). You've either got it or you don't? The stability of political interest over the life cycle. *Journal of Politics, 72*(3), 747–766. https://doi.org/10.1017/S0022381610000149

Putnam, R. D. (2000). *Bowling alone: The collapse and revival of American community*. New York: Simon and Schuster.

Purtill, J. (2016, November 10). How one million young people staying home elected Donald Trump [Text]. Retrieved from http://www.abc.net.au/triplej/programs/hack/one-million-young-people-staying-home-elected-donald-trump/8014712

Quiroz-Martinez, J., Wu, D. P., & Zimmerman, K. (2005). *ReGeneration: Young people shaping environmental justice*. Oakland, CA: Movement Strategy Center.

Randall, D. (2017). *Making citizens: How American universities teach civics*. National Association of Scholars. Retrieved from https://www.nas.org/images/documents/NAS_makingCitizens_fullReport.pdf

Report of the Committee of Five. (1908). On instruction in American government in secondary schools. *Proceedings of the American Political Science Association, 5*, 219–257.

Reynolds, H. L. (2010). Overview. In H. L. Reynolds, E. S. Brondizio, J. M. Robinson, D. Karpa, & B. L. Gross (Eds.), *Teaching environmental Literacy: Across campus and across the curriculum* (pp. 17–28). Bloomington: University of Indiana Press.

Richmond, E., Mikhail Z., & Gross, E. 2016. "Dissecting the Youth Vote." The Atlantic, November 11, 2016. Retrieved from: https://www.theatlantic.com/education/archive/2016/11/dissecting-the-youth-vote/507416/.

Rock the Vote. (2007). Young Voter Media Background. Retrieved from https://www.rockthevote.com/assets/publications/research/rtv_young_voter_myths_and_facts-2007.pdf

Rogoff, B. (2014). Learning by observing and pitching in to family and community endeavors: An orientation. *Human Development, 57*(2–3), 69–81.

Rosenstone, S. J., & Hansen, J. M. (1993). *Mobilization, participation, and democracy in America*. New York:: Macmillan.

Saez, E., & Zucman, G. (2014). *Wealth inequality in the United States since 1913: Evidence from capitalized income tax data*. National Bureau of Economic Research. Retrieved from http://www.nber.org/papers/w20625

Safi, M. (2016, March 18). Have millennials given up on democracy? *Guardian*. Retrieved from https://www.theguardian.com/world/2016/mar/18/have-Millennials-given-up-on-democracy

Schachter, H. L. (1998). Civic education: Three early American Political Science Association committees and their relevance for our times. *PS: Political Science & Politics, 31*(3), 631–635.

Schier, S. E. (2000). *By invitation only: The rise of exclusive politics in the United States*. Pittsburgh, PA: University of Pittsburgh Press.

Schudson, M. (1998). *The good citizen: A history of American civic life.* New York: Free Press.

Schwartz, A. E., Leos-Urbel, J., & Wiswall, M. (2015). *Making summer matter: The Impact of youth employment on academic performance.* National Bureau of Economic Research. Retrieved from http://www.nber.org/papers/w21470

Seipel, A. (2014, August 10). Millennial voters are paying attention—So why don't more vote? Retrieved from http://www.npr.org/sections/itsallpolitics/2014/10/08/354187589/millennial-voters-are-paying-attention-so-why-don-t-more-actually-vote

Shames, S. (2017). *Out of the running: Why millennials reject political careers and why it matters.* New York: New York University Press.

Sharkey, P. (2013). *Stuck in place: Urban neighborhoods and the end of progress toward racial equality.* Chicago: University of Chicago Press.

Sharon Statement: A timeless declaration of conservative principles. (2016). Young Americans for Freedom. Retrieved from http://www.yaf.org/news/the-sharon-statement/

Shea, D. M. (2009). Local political parties and young voters: context, resources, and policy innovation. In J. Youniss & P. Levine (Eds.), *Engaging young people in civic life* (pp. 164–184). Nashville: Vanderbilt University Press.

Shea, D. M, & Green, J. C. (2007). The turned-off generation: Fact and fiction. In D. M. Shae & J. C. Green (Eds.), *The fountain of youth: Strategies and tactics for mobilizing America's young voters* (pp. 1–18). Plymouth, UK: Rowan & Littlefield.

Shirky, C. (2008). *Here comes everybody: The power of organizing without organizations.* New York: Penguin.

Shrestha, L. B., & Heister, E. J. (2011). *The changing demographic profile of the United States.* Congressional Research Service. Retrieved from https://fas.org/sgp/crs/misc/RL32701.pdf

Sieben, I., & De Graaf, P. M. (2004). Schooling or social origin? The bias in the effect of educational attainment on social orientations. *European Sociological Review, 20*(2), 107–122.

Sigillito, S. (2016, February). Can you pass the citizenship test? Retrieved from http://www.nationalreview.com/article/414431/can-you-pass-citizenship-test-serena-sigillito

Simending, A., & Arkin, J. (2017). Why the GOP still lacks an ACA replacement plan. *Real Clear Politics.* Retrieved from http://www.realclearpolitics.com/articles'2017/01/09/why-thegop-still-lacks-an-aca-replacement-plan_132740.html

Sirianni, C. (2009). *Investing in democracy: Engaging citizens in collaborative government.* Washington, DC: Brookings Institution.

Skandera, H., & Sousa, R. (2003). *School figures: The data behind the debate.* Hoover Press. Retrieved from https://books.google.com/books?hl=en&lr=&id=_8swJODs5N0C&oi=fnd&pg=PR8&dq=School+Figures:+The+Data+Behind+the+&ots=kVgcviOfwB&sig=FtXOz84mA8VwgwHghJdDktksOoQ

Skocpol, T. (2002). Will 9/11 and the war on terror revitalize American civic democracy? *PS: Political Science and Politics, 35*(3), 537–540.

Skocpol, T. (2003). *Diminished democracy: from membership to management in American civic life.* Norman: University of Oklahoma Press.

Slaughter. A-M. & Scott, B. (2015). Rethinking the think tank: Why Washington's stuffi-est institutions need to reconnect with America, *Washington Monthly*. Retrieved from http://washingtonmonthly.com/magazine/novdec-2015/rethinking-the-think-tank/

Somin, Ilya. (2016). Democracy vs. epistocracy. Retrieved from https://www.washing-tonpost.com/news/volokh-conspiracy/wp/2016/09/03/democracy-vs-epistacracy/

Starks, L. (2017). Barack Obama and the youth vote. In L. J. Walker, F. E. Brooks, and R. B. Goings (Eds.), *How the Obama presidency changed the political landscape* (pp. 90–108). Santa Barbera: Praeger.

Steinberg, L. (2013). The influence of neuroscience on US Supreme Court decisions about adolescents' criminal culpability. *Nature Reviews Neuroscience, 14*(7), 513–518.

Stolle, D., & Cruz, C. (2005). Youth civic engagement in Canada: Implications for public policy. *Social Capital in Action, 82*, 82–144.

Stone, Chad, D. Trisi, A. Sherman, and E. Horton. "A Guide to Statistics on Historical Trends in Income Inequality." Center on Budget and Policy Priorities, November 28, 2011. https://www.cbpp.org/research/poverty-and-inequality/a-guide-to-statistics-on-historical-trends-in-income-inequality.

Taylor, Paul, and Scott Keeter. "Millennials: A Portrait of Generation next." Pew Internet & American Life Project. Washington DC: Pew Research Center, 2010. Retrieved from http://www.pewsocialtrends.org/files/2010/10/millennials-confident-connected-open-to-change.pdf.

Tienda, M. (2002). Demography and the social contract. *Demography, 39*(4), 587–616.

Tolbert, C. J., & McNeal, R. S. (2003). Unraveling the effects of the Internet on political participation? *Political Research Quarterly, 56*(2), 175–185.

Torney-Purta, J., Lehmann, R., Oswald, H., & Schulz, W. (2001). *Citizenship and educa-tion in twenty-eight countries: Civic knowledge and engagement at age fourteen.* ERIC. Retrieved from http://eric.ed.gov/?id=ED452116

The Council of Economic Advisors. (2014). 15 Economic Facts about Millennials. Retrieved from: https://obamawhitehouse.archives.gov/sites/default/files/docs/mil-lennials_report.pdf.

Turnbull, J., Root, S., Billig, S., & Jaramillo, D. (2007). *We the people.* Evaluation report. Calabas, CA: Center for Civic Education.

Twenge, J. M., Campbell, S. M., Hoffman, B. J., & Lance, C. E. (2010). Generational differences in work values: Leisure and extrinsic values increasing, social and intrin-sic values decreasing. *Journal of Management, 36*(5), 1117–1142. https://doi.org/10.1177/0149206309352246

Twenge, J. M., Campbell, W. K., & Freeman, E. C. (2012). Generational differences in young adults' life goals, concern for others, and civic orientation, 1966–2009. *Journal of Personality and Social Psychology, 102*(5), 1045.

Uricchio, C., Moore, G., & Coley, M. (2013). Corn clubs: Building the foundation for agri and extension education. *Journal of Agricultural Education, 34*(3), 224–237.

United States. Department of Homeland Security. Yearbook of Immigration Statistics: 2010. (2011). Washington, D.C.: U.S. Department of Homeland Security, Office of Immigration Statistics, 2011. retrieved from: https://www.dhs.gov/xlibrary/assets/statistics/yearbook/2010/ois_yb_2010.pdf.

Van Goethem, A., Van Hoof, A., Orobio-de Castro, B., Van Aiken, M., & Hart, D. (2015).The role of reflection in the effects of community service on adolescent development. *Child Development, 85*(6), 2114–2130.

Verba, S., Schlozman, K. L., & Brady, H. (1995). *Voice and equality: Civic voluntarism in American politics.* Cambridge, MA: Harvard University Press.

Voeten, E. (2016, December 5). That viral graph about millennials' declining support for democracy? It's very misleading. *Washington Post.* Retrieved from https://www.washingtonpost.com/news/monkey-cage/wp/2016/12/05/that-viral-graph-about-Millennials-declining-support-for-democracy-its-very-misleading/

Volunteering. (2011, July). Retrieved from http://www.childtrends.org/?indicators=volunteering

Vote view: The polarization of the Congressional Parties. http://voteview.com/political-polarization-2014.html

Wagner, M., Johann, D., & Kritzinger, S. (2012). Voting at 16: Turnout and the quality of vote choice. *Special Symposium: Generational Differences in Electoral Behaviour, 31*(2), 372–383. https://doi.org/10.1016/j.electstud.2012.01.007

Wagner, M., & Zeglovits, E. (2014). The Austrian experience shows that there is little risk and much to gain from giving 16-year-olds the vote. *British Politics and Policy at LSE.* Retrieved from http://blogs.lse.ac.uk/politicsandpolicy/voting-at-16/

Wattenberg, M. P. (2012). *Is voting for young people?* New York: Routledge.

Watts, R. J., & Flanagan C. (2007). Pushing the envelope on youth civic engagement: a developmental and liberation psychological perspective. *Journal of Community Psychology, 35*(6), 779–792.

Werner, E. (2017, February 17). McConnell intends to replace 'Obamacare' without Democrats. *PBS NewsHour.* Retrieved from http://www.pbs.org/newshour/rundown/mcconnell-intends-replace-obamacare-without-democrats/

Wessel, T., & Wessel, M. (1982). *4-H: an American idea.* Chevy Chase, MD: National 4-H Council.

Westheimer, J. (2015). *What kind of citizen? Educating our children for the common good.* New York: Teachers College Press.

Westheimer, J., & Kahne, J. (2004). What kind of citizen? The politics of educating for democracy. *American Educational Research Journal, 41*(2), 237–269.

White, L., Jr. (1967). The historical roots of our ecological crisis. *Science, 155*(3767), 1203–1207.

White House Conference on Children in a Democracy. (1942). Final report. Washington, DC: Government Printing Office. Retrieved from https://archive.org/details/finalreport00whit

Whiteley, P. (2012). Does citizenship education work? Evidence from a decade of citizenship education in secondary schools in England. *Parliamentary Affairs, 67*, 513–535.

Wilkinson, R., & Pickett, K. (2010). *The spirit level: Why greater equality makes societies stronger.* New York: Bloomsbury Press.

Wilson, E. O. (1993, May 30). Is humanity suicidal? *New York Times Magazine.*

Wilson, J. A., Acheson, J. M., Metcalfe, M., & Kleban, P. (1994). Chaos, complexity and community management of fisheries. *Marine Policy, 18*(4), 291–305.

Winograd, M., & Hais, M. D. (2011). *Millennial momentum: How a new generation is remaking America*. New Brunswick, NJ: Rutgers University Press.

Wisconsin vs. Yoder (1972). Retrieved from https://supreme.justia.com/cases/federal/us/406/205/case.html

Wogan, J. P. (2013). Takoma Park sees high turnout among teens after election reform. Governing.com. Retrieved from http://www.governing.com/news/headlines/gov-maryland-city-sees-high-turnout-among-teens-after-election-reform.html

Yates, M., & Youniss, J. (1999). *Roots of civic identity: International perspectives on community service and activism in youth*. New York: Cambridge University Press.

You.gov (2016). Republicans split by age on climate change. Retrieved from https://today.yougov.com/news/2016/02/03/republicans-split-age-climate-change/

Youniss, J. (2012). How to enrich civic education and sustain democracy. In D. E. Campbell, M Levinson, & F. M. Hess (Eds.), *Making civics count: citizenship education for a new generation* (pp 115–133). Cambridge, MA: Harvard Education Press.

Youniss, J., & Levine, P. (Eds.). (2009). *Engaging young people in civic life*. Nashville: Vanderbilt University Press.

Youniss, J., & Yates, M. (1997). *Community service and social responsibility in youth*. Chicago: University of Chicago Press.

Zaff, J., Youniss, J., & Gibson, C. (2009). *An inequitable invitation to citizenship*. Washington, DC: Philanthropy for Active Civic Engagement.

Zeglovits, E., & Aichholzer, J. (2014). Are people more inclined to vote at 16 than at 18? Evidence for the first-time voting boost among 16-to 25-year-olds in Austria. *Journal of Elections, Public Opinion and Parties, 24*(3), 351–361.

Zeglovits, E., & Zandonella, M. (2013). Political interest of adolescents before and after lowering the voting age: the case of Austria. *Journal of Youth Studies, 16*(8), 1084–1104. https://doi.org/10.1080/13676261.2013.793785

Zimmerman, S. (2014). The returns to college admission for academically marginal students. *Journal of Labor Economics, 32*(4), 711–754.

ABOUT THE AUTHORS

Daniel Hart, EdD, is Distinguished Professor of Psychology and Faculty Director of the Institute for Effective Education at Rutgers University. His research focuses on adolescent development in context. One facet of this work examines the development of civic life, including political knowledge, volunteering, social trust, and activism. In a series of studies, Hart and his colleagues have explored the effects of neighborhood, social class, and historical time on the developmental trajectories of these components of civic life.

He is also interested in the effects of different kinds of neighborhoods on personality and moral development. In this work, Hart traces the distinctive effects of neighborhood demographics—poverty, community age structure, segregation—on both configurations of personality traits within adolescents and on teenagers' moral and antisocial behaviors.

Currently, Hart is providing the technical and professional assistance for the Robert Wood Johnson Foundation's *Next Generation of Community Leaders* initiative, which funds youth-led community development projects in communities throughout New Jersey.

James Youniss, PhD, is Emeritus Professor of Psychology at the Catholic University of America, Washington, DC. He has had an active career for 57 years, studying children's and youth's normal development. For 25 years he has done research and written about youth's civic engagement, including the books *Community Service and Social Responsibility in Youth* (with Miranda Yates), *The Roots of Civic Identity* (with Miranda Yates), and *Engaging Youth in Civic Life* (with Peter Levine).

Figures are indicated by an italic *f* following the page number.

campaign management
  effect on polarization, 27–28
  failure to seek youth votes, 53–54
  money and allotment of voice in
    Congress, 20
  Obama campaign success at, 54–55
  redrawing electoral districts, 20–21
  targeted recruitment in, 56
  See also politics
Campbell, C., 73
Campbell, D. E., 6, 68–69, 74
Campbell, David, 69–70
Campbell, S. M., 51
Canada
  4-H program participation in, 99
  interest among teens in voting, 75
  requirement for youth community
    service, 75
Cannan, J., 23
Carney, E. N., 19
Casey, B. J., 119–120
Caughey, D., 27
Chan, T. W., 118
Chappell, E., 59, 60
Chesapeake Bay area, 96
Chetty, R., 66–67
Chilton, D., 47
Chin, M., 71
Christopher Columbus Foundation, 93
Cinner, J., 91
CIRCLE (Center for Information,
  Research and Civic Learning and
  Education), 7, 54
citizen identity, 74, 127
citizens and citizenship
  engaged citizenship, 10, 84–85, 84*f*
  implications of group membership, 85,
    127–130
  polarization among, 24–27
  shifting meaning of, 83–84
  smarter model of a good citizen, 11–12
  voting as an entitlement, 102–104
Citizens United decision, 31
Civic and Political Health Survey
  (CPHS), 84

civic development
  in 21st century, 12–13, 123–136
  causes of increased interest in, 7–8,
    9*f*, 39–40
  changing organization structure and,
    85, 127–130
  demographic and economic transitions
    challenging, 124–127
  difficulty in advancing, 87–88
  effect on voting, 135–136
  engaging youth in, 132–135
  media as a solution, 54–55, 130–132
  need to promote among youth, 123–124
  providing young Americans opportuni-
    ties for, 11–13, 56–57, 87–88
  shifting meaning of citizenship
    and, 83–84
  through environmental
    engagement, 87–100
Civic Mission of Schools, The (Levine and
  Gibson), 6
civic organizations, 85, 127–130
civics education
  approaches to enhancement, 6–7
  civics-in-action education, 74–80
  concern over curriculum, 64–65
  efficacy of, 5–6, 65–69, 73–74
  goals of, 80–86
  by informed discussion, 69–71
  by interactions with students, 62–63
  "new civics," 3–4
  personal values of teachers and, 72–73
  as responsibility of schools, 61–62
  state requirements concerning, 69
  strategies for effective, 11–12. *see
    also* civics-in-action education;
    environmental civics
  by transmitting civics knowledge, 63–64
civics-in-action education
  activity selection, 78–79
  civic disposition of students
    and, 79–80
  efforts by public commissions to
    advance, 77–78
  England's approach to, 76–77